ART*iculating*

ARTiculating

Teaching Writing in a Visual World

PAMELA B. CHILDERS

ERIC H. HOBSON

JOAN A. MULLIN

Boynton/Cook Publishers
HEINEMANN
Portsmouth, NH

BOYNTON/COOK PUBLISHERS, INC.
A subsidiary of Reed Elsevier Inc.
361 Hanover Street
Portsmouth, NH 03801–3912

Offices and agents throughout the world

The authors and publisher wish to thank those who have generously given permission to reprint borrowed material:

On the cover: Winslow Homer, *The Blue Boy*; Ball State University Museum of Art, Muncie, Indiana, Elisabeth Ball Collection, partial gift and promised gift of the George and Frances Ball Foundation; 95.036.15

On page 26, Thomas Eakins, *Shad Fishing at Gloucester-on-the-Delaware*; Ball State University Museum of Art, Muncie, Indiana, Elisabeth Ball Collection, partial gift and promised gift of the George and Frances Ball Foundation; 95.036.10

Library of Congress Cataloging-in-Publication Data
Childers, Pamela B., 1943–
    ARTiculating : teaching writing in a visual world / Pamela B.
Childers, Eric H. Hobson, Joan A. Mullin.
        p.   cm.
    Includes bibliographical references.
    ISBN 0–86709–442–7
    1. English language—Rhetoric—Study and teaching.
2. Interdisciplinary approach in education.   3. Report writing—
Study and teaching.   4. Visual perception.   5. Art in education.
I. Hobson, Eric.   II. Mullin, Joan A., 1949–   .   III. Title.
PE1404.C48   1998
808'.042'07—dc21   97–48387
                                                    CIP

EDITOR: *Peter R. Stillman*
PRODUCTION: *Vicki Kasabian*
COVER DESIGN: *Jenny Jensen Greenleaf*
MANUFACTURING: *Louise Richardson*

Printed in the United States of America on acid-free paper

02   01   00   99   98   RRD   1   2   3   4   5

In memory of
Dennis C. Myers (1940–1995),
who helped us articulate our visions of the world

Contents

Preface

At the 1996 NCTE Board of Directors' meeting in Chicago, the following resolution passed by an overwhelming majority:

> RESOLVED, that the National Council of Teachers of English through its publications, conferences, and affiliates support professional development and public awareness of the role that viewing and visually representing our world have as a form of literacy. (99)

The interesting part of the floor discussion before the vote was not whether the visual was important but whether "visual" should be paired with "literacy." A colleague proposed amending the resolution by dropping the word "literacy," although he admitted that perhaps he was being too traditional, and the ensuing barrage of comments indicated that he was. It soon became clear that many of our colleagues in secondary schools and colleges already incorporate elements of visual literacy in their writing and literature classes, that they know the importance of the visual in an increasingly computerized multimedia culture, and that they worry about whether they are adequately equipped to teach their students about the intersections between the visual and the verbal. They voted for the resolution because they wanted to make more explicit the need to address the visual and the need for more instructional resources. In this book we hope to address those concerns in concrete ways.

For years, many of us have used paintings, photographs, and other forms of illustrative material from particular historical periods to provide a specific context for our students. Some of us ask students to observe and write about a parking lot, a car, their bedroom, or an orange, all in an attempt to teach description, comparison/contrast, or process. Another still popular form of analysis calls for a textual reading of a magazine or TV advertisement in order to identify how the print and visual elements collaborate to produce a desired response (intellectual, emotional, visceral) in a specific audience. In other instances, we deconstruct the media to expose how discordant and oddly juxtaposed images often convey covert, subversive messages. A similar writing task involves analyzing a TV

show, a commercial, or a talk show. While these useful and enter-
taining activities are valuable in stimulating writing, more often
than not they remain small pieces of a much larger syllabus or curriculum that focuses exclusively on the verbal, relegating the visual
to second place. For this reason, we offer specific strategies and ways
of thinking about the relationship(s) between the visual and verbal
realms of communication that more fully recognize their connections, and we examine and use them in our writing—and, by extension, in every—classroom.

We base this book on three premises:

1. In the development of literacy, as in life experiences, image pre-
   cedes language.

2. We live in an increasingly visual world.

3. Teaching practices can capitalize on visual pedagogical connections to improve learning.

Some of the chapters point to a small part of the ever-increasing, multidisciplinary literature now available in the visual literacy area; but in
general, we have chosen to present actual practices in language and
visual learning, since these inspire further research specific to our
own practices and disciplines. To emphasize the need to examine our
disciplinary objective, the activities described also demonstrate how to
adapt language and visual arts pedagogy across disciplines and how
much we can learn from the practices of other disciplines. Since language learning is the key to all disciplinary meaning making, we have
included two guest-written chapters, one describing how content
leads writing, even in a writing classroom, and another showing how
writing enlarges understanding of content. Both chapters rely on visual content, and both demonstrate how such content can motivate
students' performance and their engagement.

The chapter activities lead students to the sources of their writing
and language abilities (metaphors, mental images, problem-solving
algorithms, culturally coded responses). These visual-verbal practices
are also consistent with current domain research to allow students access to information in accordance with their dominant and preferred
styles of learning. Students come to understand how to use the visual
productively for their own benefit as well as to communicate within
specific environments for specific purposes. While the visual activities
meet student-specific objectives, the chapters also provide teachers
across the curriculum and at many educational levels with strategies
that employ visual-based pedagogy to connect classroom learning objectives with larger curricular learning objectives.

The book is meant to be used as a guide, a catalyst, and a prompt.

We suggest that you jot responses in the margins, on blank pages, or in your own journals, sketchbooks, or notebooks as we did in reading each other's chapters. We make our reactions explicit in the commentary following each chapter. In these supplementary sections, we wanted to exemplify how those specifically trained to apply writing techniques across the disciplines can transfer visual techniques to their classes and those of their colleagues. We invite you to do the same.

In Chapter 1, Eric Hobson establishes many of the themes that reappear throughout the text and expands on our major premises:

1. Writing and the arts (broadly defined) share much in their approaches to composing and manipulating the messages unique to their discourse communities.

2. Teachers of writing should adopt methods employed by teachers in other disciplines in order to expand their understanding of the kinds of communication contexts in which students must operate.

3. The affective dimension, represented in part by teachers' and students' personality preferences and predominant learning styles, plays a vital role in education processes.

In Chapter 2, Joe Trimmer takes a common activity in the English language arts classroom and turns it—and the structure of the class—on end. Who hasn't used a picture of a painting as a stimulus to writing? But how many of us have used postcards, the quintessential linking of picture and word, to engage students in a whole course of reading, writing, researching, and speaking? With its emphasis on collaboration and its student-centered pedagogy, this classroom-focused chapter shows how we can breathe new life into some of the visuals and writing practices we may already use.

If Trimmer's article moves students from the classroom to the museum, in Chapter 3, Pam Childers reverses the process. Again, it is not uncommon for teachers to turn to a museum or a similar resource for student learning, but what do you do once you have the students in the building? Not only does this chapter offer suggestions for actively engaging students in observing and writing, it goes further to focus on using art to motivate those who may be more visual (or metaphoric) than their verbal peers. Through her emphasis on student drawing and poetry, Childers shows that "All subject matter benefits from placing it within a visual and/or cultural context."

Chapter 4 moves from inside the museum and its art collections to a multipurpose discussion of the building itself. When she was team teaching a course in postmodern architecture, Joan Mullin found that students tended to write boring, formulaic, unsupported papers about the buildings they were studying. Part of the problem was the difficulty of learning the vocabulary of architecture, but there was also the fact that students couldn't or wouldn't break away from their narrow views of how they thought a paper should look. She asked students to describe the *footprint* of two very different buildings (including a tour) and then had them compare these buildings to two different ways of structuring papers. Not only did students learn how to write, Mullin argues, they also learned the subject matter. The chapter further suggests, however, that this use of buildings transfers most successfully to writing classes where a physical tour helps students internalize the integration of written structure, organization, transition, audience, and content.

Moving away from the writing and art history class, Chapter 5 examines the use of visuals across the secondary and postsecondary curriculum. Building on her experience as a nationally recognized resource person for writing-across-the-curriculum (WAC) programs, Pam Childers describes how a visual-verbal approach to writing can open doors and inform instruction in areas such as art, biology, history, mathematics, English as a second language (ESL), and English. The discussion for each subject area presents classroom-based activities and assignments designed to foster students' ability to use multi-sensory/visual-verbal approaches to problem-solving and writing.

Following on the writing perspective of earlier chapters, Richard Putney, our second guest author, shows in Chapter 6 how observing, creating visuals, and responding to them in writing can teach content in a history course or in any class where cultural contexts open a way into learning course material. His course on the monuments of Gettysburg values the iconography and sculpture of the late 1800s, but it also helps students to see how attitudes toward the Civil War, toward death, and toward monuments shape what we see—and how we interpret what we see—today.

Chapter 7 moves students a step closer to understanding how our communities and our times shape our knowledge and our interpretation of the world. In an attempt to capitalize on a personal preference for associating names with visual cues, Joan Mullin discovered a valuable way to motivate and involve students in their own and in other's construction of the world. Her method uses crayons, colored pens and pencils, wrapping paper, ribbon, glitter glue, and various other pieces of stuff that might seem more appropriate to an elementary school activity, but it was devised specifically for college students of all ages. Mullin's classroom practice allows students to access content by employing their various individual learning styles, teaches students about content, audience, and interpretation, and, finally, creates a sense of community. It was recently (and successfully) tried with a high school class.

Finally, in Chapter 8 Eric Hobson leads readers through a faculty development workshop that explores the use of the visual in instruction. The exercises he presents transfer successfully to the classroom and will give students various options for navigating the often frustrating invention, development, and revision stages of writing. Readers can participate by jotting reactions and notes on a separate sheet of paper. They can also invite their colleagues to think about how these activities can stimulate learning in their classrooms.

In the materials that accompanied the NCTE resolution passed in Chicago, the resolution committee wrote that "Teachers and students need to expand their appreciation of how people gather and share their information. Teachers should guide students in constructing meaning through creating and viewing nonprint texts." We fervently believe that this also applies to us. As the resolution committee eloquently stated, "To participate in a global society, we continue extending our ways of communicating. Viewing and visually representing (defined in the NCTE/IRA Standards for English Language Arts) are a part of our growing consciousness of how people gather and share information." We invite readers to share ideas with us and with colleagues, because we hope to continue making hands-on activities like these available as we face our increasingly visual future together.

Acknowledgments

The idea for this book developed from a workshop planned over drinks and food at the 1993 Conference on College Composition and Communication (CCCC) in San Diego. Each of us had been exploring, tinkering with, thinking about, or writing about the connections between the visual and the written before these informal dialogues occurred. As each of us discussed our experiences with the issue, we fell into a Judy Garland–Mickey Rooney scenario ("Let's put on a show!"). Pam put the show together—a workshop proposal for the next CCCC in Nashville—by asking Joan and Eric what they wanted to do. We want to thank Joe Trimmer and Malcolm Childers for their part in those early conversations and that first workshop.

After four years of collaborating on workshops and conference panels with colleagues from around the country and the world, we have discovered that we are not alone in making connections between the visual world and teaching writing. We want to thank our workshop participants because their emotional involvement and commitment, and the wealth of ideas we gathered, convinced us that this book had to happen. Through further presentations, workshops, and interactions with others interested in our research, we started to put the book together.

We cannot overlook the ways our thinking and writing have been influenced by workshop participants who have kept in contact with us and by colleagues and students who continue to touch our visual and writing souls and who, like R. Baird Shuman, Lida Cochran, and Richard Putney, routinely route materials our way.

In more ways than we can begin to count, we also thank Malcolm Childers for the behind-the-scenes role he played in bringing this project to completion. For years he has visually dazzled us with his relief etchings and photographs, entertained us with his music and poetry, fed us, and kept our humor—and good sense—intact over long planning and writing sessions in and around his studio atop Signal Mountain outside Chattanooga. In addition, we thank those colleagues and friends who listened to our ideas and read our early attempts to articulate them, particularly Carla J. McDonough and Steven E. Reno.

We also want to acknowledge the importance of our involvement in voluntary professional organizations such as the National Council of Teachers of English and CCCC. Both have been supportive of our proposals for conferences, and CCCC took a real risk in allowing us two half-day workshops before and after the Milwaukee conference so attendees could use photographs they collected during the conference. We applaud these organizations for realizing the importance of exploring new territory and for supporting us as lifelong learners, educators, and humanists.

As is true of so many others in this book, Peter Stillman's visual world is permanently connected to his writing—and to ours. We wish to thank him for his encouragement on this project, for his personal and professional commitment to us, and for his critical eye. Any remaining errors only testify to our continual need to re-vision the world.

Graphic art cannot be totally separated from literary art, nor vice versa. They encroach on each other.
—ARNOLD BENNETT

Seeing Writing in a Visual World

ERIC H. HOBSON

I do not recall any professor with whom I studied while pursuing the Ph.D. in composition discussing composition from any perspective other than that of the production of written texts. The focus of these discussions was always the construction of writing: not art, not music, not mathematics and other symbol systems. The anecdotal evidence about their training we have gathered from colleagues in the field of writing suggests that these omissions are the norm. What can be perceived as a type of academic myopia is not unique to the composition community. Witnessing the same thing in her discipline, Janet Olson, an art educator and the author of *Envisioning Writing: Toward an Integration of Drawing and Writing* (1992), suggests one of many viable explanations for this academic provincialism when she laments that "With each step of specialization teachers become more limited in their understanding of other subjects and their relation to the teachers' own areas of expertise. Their understanding of students' educational development also suffers, since their observation and judgment are informed by a narrow frame of reference, both in terms of time spent with students and in terms of their disciplinary expertise" (148).

Such a restricted field of vision should not be surprising, however. In fact, as we note throughout this book, discussions of the similarities between the composing processes in the arts and in other disciplines are relatively few and far between. Even rarer are attempts to translate these similarities to provide teachers and students with additional and alternative strategies for entering into the complex problem-solving activity of creating and crafting written texts. Having studied and collaborated with artists who work in many mediums, we believe the linkages that connect the composing processes they manipulate to create their work seem absurdly obvious (Hobson 1990).

Thankfully, we do not make this argument in complete isolation. R. Baird Shuman and Denny Wolfe, for instance, summarize the thesis of their NCTE monograph, *Teaching English Through the Arts* (1990), in the following way:

> Our point here is that writing is like all the other arts in this regard: all are composing activities and therefore require invention. Just as composition in speaking and writing has to do with ordering words, so composition in music has to do with ordering sound, and drawing or painting has to do with ordering objects in space, and so on. All forms of composition assist in the process of clarifying and ordering thought and feeling, in creating and understanding concepts—in short, in learning. All of us hope that our students will learn to think critically and creatively. But to do so, they must have practice. Involving students in the arts both ensures that practice and expands its variety. (7)

Likewise, Olson (1992) writes that "Since children are both visual and verbal learners, and since both images and words are effective and compatible tools for communication, it seems obvious that the two should never be separated. Unfortunately, the traditional understanding of the visual image has been far too narrow and greatly misunderstood by most language-arts teachers" (45). Taking a narrower focus than that of either Shuman and Wolfe or Olson, Catherine Golden (1986), in "Composition: Writing and the Visual Arts," explores correlations between the composing processes used by painters and those used by writers: "I think there are useful parallels between the genesis of a painting and that of a written manuscript. The artist's first simple sketch seems to function like a writer's verbal map or outline, similarly capturing the central theme of the composition: the initial vision. Early sketches or studies for a painting are like drafts for a written composition. Both show a way of progressing from initial vision to completed composition" (60).

Along with Shuman and Wolfe, Olson, and Golden, and others, we adhere to this statement: *"Writing's 'composing process' is closely related to the operational processes that fuel successful creation in other areas."* For us, this is just common sense. Karen Ernst (1994) explains and justifies her long-standing efforts to use writing to improve elementary students' art, and art to improve their writing, in her description of the educational environment she strives to create. It is one in which "pictures as well as language would be part of the continuum of forming—that is, meaning making" (8). This integrated understanding of how students can and do use multiple media to help them make meaning out of their surrounding world, however, garners scant attention within the written composition community, particularly at levels directly affecting secondary and postsecondary instruction. Coupled with our professional obligation to teach students to write more successfully (that is, to create academic prose), this oversight helps maintain a chasm between the site-specific, nitty-gritty truths about composing we have learned from experience and the more abstract musings and teachings of the academic community.

Writing Is a Visual Art

Writing developed as a *visual* means of communication (Coulmas 1988; Harris 1986; Jean 1992; Olson 1992; Shuman and Wolfe 1990), and a long, continuing history of close incorporation of visual elements in many different text forms has been maintained. Illustrated manuscripts, calligraphy, and tapestries are but a few of the art forms in which distinctions between word and form are blurred to the point of meaninglessness. In discussing calligraphy, Olson (1992) reminds us that "The calligraphic (meaning 'words written by hand') form of these characters is itself a legitimate and widely appreciated visual art form. Calligraphy incorporates all the elements of a painting—line, shape, texture, unity, balance, rhythm, proportion—all within its own unique form of composition" (131).

Given this history, the distance between the visual and the verbal forms of information practiced in verbal-based classrooms is highly artificial. Focusing on the linkages between the composing processes employed in the arts as well as on their similar histories, Shuman and Wolfe (1990) draw what they see as "two pertinent conclusions":

- Early composition that was used as a means of preserving and transmitting ideas and information through the ages took the forms of *singing* and *drawings*.
- Early alphabetic writing was an art form that may have had less to do with composing the content of what was to be communicated than with the art form itself.

"Obviously," they conclude, "connections between language and the arts have roots deep in antiquity" (2). Olson too finds these connections worth exploring. Discussing the development of writing, she notes that the "Greeks chose to represent each spoken sound with a symbol (or letter). But what is most important about this transition is that all of these writing forms and systems were originally picture drawings. Because phonetical representation was viewed as an important advancement, the significant role the picture played in this achievement often went unnoticed. Just as speech developed out of the imitation of sound, writing developed out of the imitation of forms of real objects or beings. At the beginning of all writing stands the picture" (130).

Given the current interest in stressing interdisciplinary approaches within educational activity at all levels, primary through postsecondary, the present is a particularly opportune moment to attempt many of the instructional approaches presented and implied in the following pages. As is readily evident from the projects described, for instance, by Joe Trimmer (see Chapter 2) and Joan Mullin (see Chapter 7), the cross-disciplinary synergy that results from integrating the visual and the verbal in our teaching can be quite invigorating. What is not as foregrounded in these particular discussions, however, are other benefits that we believe are as important, if not more important in helping students develop the critical and communicative abilities they need to function in our visually intensive culture. Richard Putney's discussion (Chapter 6) shows that initiatives such as these also create active learning environments in which integrated activities are geared to developing synthetic critical thinking and communication skills.

Consider the following statement:

> The artistic antecedent of writing, then, is drawing; the artistic antecedents of literature are songs, oral stories, improvisations, and other informal means of "acting out." Given these artistic antecedents and their history stretching through eons, it seems clear that the collective unconscious of human beings is rooted in artistic archetypes. . . . English teachers who are aware of these archetypes and who find ways to tie their teaching to them will likely open learning possibilities for students that might otherwise remain closed. (Shuman and Wolfe 1990, 8)

Question: If the connections between visual and verbal learning exist, the current educational environment is open to such integrative innovation, and this integration brings with it a host of other, linked benefits, *how* can teachers of written composition integrate these arts into their teaching when they are not masters of these other artistic media?

Answer: Easily, at least when and if we admit our amateur status in these areas and approach them as colearners with our students, since by doing so we reduce our performance anxiety and increase the chances that this exploration may be enjoyable; establish links with people whose proficiencies lie in these other arts and use them as resources.

Potential results:

Useful:	Employing the practices in this book increases the variety of activities that can prompt student writing
More useful:	Using visually based activities encourages the participation of students who are visual learners
Most useful:	Integrating the arts into the writing class can help many students learn how to ▪ discover ideas ▪ organize information ▪ overcome writer's block

Realizing these potentials within traditional writing courses and within traditional, discipline-based curricula, however, requires work, a willingness to take risks, and, most important, a desire to make new discoveries about our students' abilities and our own.

Shifting Teachers' Paradigms

In leading faculty development workshops that explore the relationships between and the transferability of the composing processes employed in writing and in the visual arts, I frequently ask participants to begin with the following task (see Chapter 8 for the complete workshop script). In order to fully appreciate its effectiveness, please complete Activity 1 before you continue reading.

Writing teachers in particular often find this task difficult at first because we tend to think verbally not visually; link metaphor to language, not to shapes and tones; use pen and pencil to generate words, not lines; and experience high levels of anxiety and insecurity when faced with unfamiliar tasks.

Activity 1

TASK:	Draw a representation of the most difficult student you have ever taught.
TIME:	5 minutes
TIPS:	Sketch quickly
	Trust your instincts
	Relax (no one else has to see your drawing)
GOAL:	Try to draw so that two days from now you can recognize the result as student X.

Because of the brief time allowed to complete this task, the drawings are usually not particularly well developed—stick figures and amoebalike entities abound. In most cases, the picture is not recognizable to anyone but the artist, but given the subjectivity of the act of representation, a high level of idiosyncrasy is to be expected. Drawings such as the one in Figure 1–1 are the norm.

In addition, the artists encounter a marked level of initial frustration, which is quickly followed by the realization that it will be impossible for them to complete the activity to their own aesthetic satisfaction. Comments such as the following are also common:

"I don't know what you want."
"I don't have sufficient time to draw well."
"Why are we drawing? I thought this was a workshop about teaching writing."
"My drawing doesn't look like anything anyone else could recognize."
"I've never been any good at drawing."

Usual Participant Assumptions

I introduce this risky activity at workshops because it brings into high relief a number of assumptions about writing and its relationship to the arts. These assumptions often include such beliefs (frequently tacitly held) as the following:

- For drawings to be valuable, they must be good (that is, aesthetically pleasing).

- Successful artistic production is a mysterious process accessible to only a select few.

Figure 1–1
"My most difficult student"

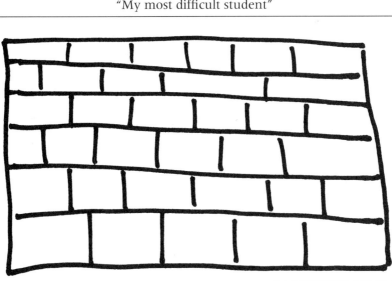

- Artistic production in the plastic and graphic arts is distinctly different (and, less academically viable) than verbal production. As such, it
  - doesn't intersect with language arts instruction in important ways
  - offers few opportunities for helping a broad range of students develop successful written composing processes
  - opens writing instruction to the perception that it is methodologically soft

These perceptions are understandable for a number of reasons. The romantic tradition in Western culture has elevated artistic production—activities outside the day-to-day, vocationally linked manipulation of print, metals, paints, video, music, and so on—to a realm reserved for a talented elite. It is hardly surprising that few people, other than those who consider themselves adept at these media, are aware of the processes used by practitioners in creating their work. This lack of awareness, among other things, disinclines us to see similarities in the composing processes that help to energize these artistic endeavors.

There is a long-standing, deeply ingrained suspicion in the United States toward high culture as somehow anti-egalitarian and even undemocratic. Art forms frequently associated with and used as markers of social class (for example, opera, classical music, painting, sculpture, and literature) simultaneously attract and repel the American psyche. The art museum is one venue in which this phenomenon is undeniable: people feel obligated to undertake a pilgrimage there but experience a sense of alienation once they arrive. The American ambivalence toward art is easily witnessed in everything from screwball comedies to cartoons to jokes told on the job. Both of these perceptions—art is the domain of a talented few; art marks and maintains social status—reveal just how tightly our culture holds to a utilitarian view. The role of *artistic expression in our everyday lives is very small.*

At the same time, the emphasis of American secondary and postsecondary education is decidedly vocational. Curricula are crafted and assessed according to whether or not graduates get jobs upon completing their course of study. Although there is continual brouhaha among the general populace over the need for students to engage in a learning process that will serve them for years and stimulate them to become lifelong learners, the vast majority of classroom practices focus on vocational utility: "Does what goes on in the classroom have a direct, one-to-one correlation to activities found in the workplace?" This is a very real and very powerful controlling question. Because the links between verbal and rhetorical fluency and visual acumen have not been consistently championed, classroom instruction that attempts not only to demonstrate this link but also to engage students in its exploration are viewed with suspicion.

An essential, although often ignored, part of the vocational focus of American education arises from the culture's faith in the promise of the scientific model to supply irrefutable answers to all problems and to prescribe definite courses of redemptive or remediative action in order to alleviate these problems. In this educational model, one methodically isolates, identifies, and categorizes the essential elements of everything from biological to linguistic systems in order to ascertain how these pieces constitute the whole system. While such an inquiry strategy is powerful, it tends to be myopic, ignoring some variables as too tangential to warrant further exploration.

This tendency to ignore those parts of the puzzle that may not make immediate and objective sense contributes, I believe, to the stranglehold that content-centered teaching (in its most limited sense) maintains on American education. What we hope to demonstrate in the following chapters is the strong, even essential, role that visual literacy plays in the development of students' writing abilities. Our students need to develop the verbal-visual skills that will enable them to write with the rhetorical sophistication they need to succeed in the undeniably visual culture that has come charging to the forefront in the closing decades of the twentieth century—and that shows no sign of retreating.

My Assumptions

Like the participants, I too enter the visual workshop with a set of preconceptions that help to determine the workshop's purpose and format. My decision to begin the workshop with the "draw student X" activity, for example, is based on several assumptions:

- The structure of most typical writing classes unwittingly privileges and by extension may exclude specific learning styles and personality profiles.
- Many students identified as "difficult" are so labeled less because of any behavioral or intellectual deficiencies than because they don't quite fit a typical or ideal student mold.

Olson's observations about the different strengths students bring to learning situations provide a link between these assumptions:

> It is a well-documented fact that 15 percent or more of all children do not respond well to verbal instruction, and many more children have varying degrees of difficulty with it. A value chart could be used to visualize these many variations. If white represents visual learners and black represents verbal learners, it's easy to see how many variations of gray are possible within the two extremes. The children who respond poorly to verbal instruction may very well be the children who simply cannot or will not pay attention, who will not lead or participate in class discussions, who seem unable or unwilling to follow directions, and who are very likely to be classified as being daydreamers, discipline problems, learning disabled, or all of the above. (5–6)

I start with this drawing activity on purpose. It is, I believe, synonymous with many assignments we give our students to tackle in that it is abstract, it has no immediate link to the workshop topic, and it presents few criteria to serve as guides and anchors. Indeed, given the expectations and preconceptions participants bring with them, the activity doesn't make a whole lot of sense. Yet I present this task to teachers because it serves as a corollary to the position in which many of their students find themselves when they receive a writing assignment. I am convinced that many of the assignments and activities presented to students in composition classes give them very real challenges because these tasks take students away from their familiar ways of discovering, exploring, revising, and articulating their ideas.

Not only do we frustrate them, but we also ask them to take risks, and taking risks is not something they are eager to do, because they know the educational system does not usually reward risk takers. How then do we go about creating an environment in which students will take the risks necessary to draw on their visual literacy in their attempts to articulate their thinking through writing?

By exposing this baggage at the start, I believe it much more likely that teachers whose instructional responsibilities lie in the verbal territories of writing and literature will *see* the workshop's central point, that the composing process in writing is similar to the composing processes in the other arts and *leave* the workshop more willing to incorporate visually based activities in their writing courses. In other words, among other secondary agendas, the workshop has the important goal of beginning a discussion of the following statements:

- Typical writing classes simultaneously privilege some and exclude other available composition tools.
- Many writing classes consider invention and revision exclusively within a verbal framework.
- Many writing teachers assume that the majority of their students encounter and process reality exactly as they themselves do.
- These approaches stymie students' abilities.

Building a Bridge Between the Visual and the Verbal

True or False:

_____ Writing classes do not hold most students enthralled.
_____ Writing classes do not send most students into states of rapture.
_____ Writing classes are often extremely frustrating experiences for students.

I doubt that many experienced English teachers would argue with these statements. One reason they ring true is that they are deeply rooted in contemporary student culture, which

- sees student-teacher relationships as adversarial
- approves a cool pose of indifference toward learning
- values students' egocentric determination of what in their education is important
- penalizes taking risks in front of peers

Less easily dismissed, however, are a number of important factors that can lead to potentially erroneous assumptions about levels of student motivation and ability.

In my own case, as a student I tended to doodle in my notebooks more than I took notes during class. This behavior bothered several of my teachers so much, they expressed concern about my study habits. One professor—my undergraduate advisor—even recommended that I enroll in a study skills course to learn how to take effective notes. These teachers were operating within a verbally determined conceptual framework. Within their paradigm of learning, note taking—the recording/transcribing of course content using words and/or shorthand notations—was a necessary component for success within the discipline. What these teachers did not understand was that as a learner, I am quite visually dependent. I learn best and am most comfortable when I can *see* relationships between ideas tangibly illustrated and *watch* task performances modeled.

When I attempted to perform as a dutiful English student by taking copious notes, I found that I focused less on the information being presented than on the act of taking notes. The net result was that while I had nice notes, I didn't really have the contextual framework I needed to make more complete sense out of them. When I returned to my notes to review course material, I just couldn't get the *feel* of them; I'd come away from reading them frustrated. For me, as a visual learner,

class notes (transcribed words) ≠ optimal learning

Part of the problem, I realized, was that while taking notes, my attention was centered on the page, not on the teacher and the class interaction. While doodling, however, my vision and hearing were focused almost exclusively on the teacher and the class discussion. The marks I made included key data from the day's activity (names, dates, key words), geometric forms with suggested linkages, and cartoonish images of teachers, classmates, and items in the room. This mélange of images provided me a rich palette of visual and mnemonic cues. Through them I could reenter the class environment and recall in fine detail much of what was said—and what was stressed—during lectures and discussions.

This type of learning experience is not completely idiosyncratic. Karen Ernst, for example, describes several such moments in *Picturing Learning: Artists and Writers in the Classroom* (1994). "My use of drawing and writing in my research journal was central to my observation of and communication with students," she writes. "Drawing was a way for me to take field notes and was an essential part of my teaching and research" (25):

Drawing Allen and Martin as they wrote in their artists notebooks focused my concentration, enabling me to be present for their work in the classroom, to record both the experience and the context. Words and pictures worked in partnership as tools to describe meaning. (31)

My writing and drawing worked as partners as I drew Brenda, robed in her green striped smock, working at her table on her painting. I focused on her painting, and that led me to interview her; her words filled the spaces around the drawing. For me, recording the words with the drawing captured the moment. (31)

Toby Gordon, in "Drawing My Selves Together: An Editor's Notebook" (Hubbard and Ernst 1996), echoes these experiences:

when I want it, I have room to roam. On the phone, in meetings, at conferences, I decorate, doodle, make the pages visually appealing. While talking with authors and colleagues, I let my pen go. My hand stays busy, and my listening becomes more active and acute. Their words, and my thinking about their words, fill up the pages. Faces, figures, and designs float in the margins. And later my words and images—as inaccurate as they may be—will bring me right back to the precise moment of a long-ago meeting, conversation, or conference. The tone of the moment lingers in the white space. I can't lose it now. And from there I can turn it around, play with it, hold it; I can recapture old feelings and generate new ideas. (153)

Put simply, there is no perfect, universal way to learn. In most writing classes, however, one could easily conclude otherwise: much of the interaction takes place exclusively in words. Teachers give students with assignments and content information orally, sometimes supplemented with printed materials, and students provide teachers with print-only texts. This situation stacks the learning deck—and, by extension, the assessment deck—in ways that enable select groups of students to succeed while other groups flounder. It can be argued that group membership is determined by students' learning styles, which, when mixed with a teacher's presentation style linked to his or her preferred ways of learning, create classroom environments in which a minority of students feel completely comfortable while a majority experience increasing levels of discomfort and dissonance.

The question of how learning styles influence and even determine how one learns is nothing new to the education literature. Inventories such as the Myers Briggs Type Inventory (MBTI) and Howard Gardner's (1983) multiple intelligences provide students and teachers with a descriptive apparatus for discussing and understanding how they best interact with the world. For classroom applications, however, these tools are often quite cumbersome. In addition to their administration costs, they confront students with pages of questions that often require them to choose between options they employ with equal ease.

To overcome these limitations, Fleming and Mills (1992) created a thirteen-question survey (VARK inventory) to help students identify their own dominant learning style and to offer them study strategies designed to augment that style. The VARK inventory focuses on four learning styles:

- Visual (V): preference for graphical and symbolic ways of representing information
- Aural (A): preference for "heard" information
- Read/Write (R): preferences for information printed as words
- Kinesthetic (K): preference to the use of experience and practice (simulated or real) (140)

This inventory highlights the fact that students do not bring the same learning strategies and abilities to the classroom; rather, they exhibit markedly different preferences for interacting with new information and new concepts, employing more than the reading, writing, and listening skills traditionally valued by teachers. While the authors provide no information about how these styles are typically distributed across student populations, there are marked similarities between the students described in their discussions and the types of learners coming out of Olson's (1992) classroom observations as an art teacher and teacher trainer. She argues that a class usually includes "four basic types of students, each type representing approximately 25 percent of the class":

Type A. High visual and high verbal skills

Type B. High visual and low verbal skills

Type C. Low visual and high verbal skills

Type D. Low visual and low verbal skills

She describes each group and discusses how an integrated visual-verbal method of writing instruction benefits each. Type A students excel at all tasks and find the simultaneous use of visual and verbal skills challenging. Type B students "have great difficulty with the normal academic tasks that are basically verbal" and do not achieve high levels of academic success; however, "these are the students who benefit most from the visual-verbal method of writing and are most likely to show dramatic improvement." Type C students get good grades and view visual activities as "a waste of time" yet can benefit from visually based instruction, because it stretches their preconceptions and offers options they would not otherwise recognize. Type D students are those whose chances of academic success are remote but for whom drawing is more concrete and understandable than other forms of instruction (43–44).

When I look at a group of students in terms of how their learning styles might explain the levels of success they encounter in my writing classes, I experience mixed feelings of justification and self-indictment. On the one hand, I find it reassuring that the grade distribution that I have come to expect (not dissimilar to a bell curve) can be explained by Olson's approach to the abilities and talents students bring with them. I wonder if there is anything about writing I can teach the small group of students at the high end of the performance chart. Occasionally, I encounter students whose apparent lack of talent and ability makes me question what they are doing in my college-level writing classes. In the middle are the bulk of my students, who bring with them a range of talents and abilities that by the end of the semester, place them in the middle of the pack. I present students with an opportunity to learn more about writing; what they make of that opportunity is up to them.

On the other hand, discussions of students' performance that acknowledge the role of their learning styles and teachers' learning and presentation styles in students' performance give me pause. They keep me honest about the biases built into my own classes and encourage me to explore ways of integrating information-processing and problem-solving strategies from the visual arts. I am convinced that it levels the playing field while enabling most students to experience equally powerful and productive learning. The more I think about how I taught in the past, the more sure I am that the students who came out on top were those most like the stereotypical English or humanities major. That thought drives my current thinking; it is my albatross.

Conclusion

Students who learn best by listening or by reading stand the greatest chance of doing well in school. Yet every class also includes students like me, whose visual inclinations manifest themselves in an aversion to systematic note taking. These students sit in writing courses without appearing to follow the lesson as do their "more successful," verbally oriented peers. When teachers who hold tightly to the written word as the most powerful learning medium encounter doodlers and daydreamers, it is easy for them to reach the same logical conclusion my advisor did: *These students are goofing off.*

If the research on differences in learning styles and writing is as accurate as it is convincing (Jensen and DiTibberio 1989), there is a good chance that these "lollygagging" students may in fact be on task. Drawing allowed me to interact with the class activity and material with efficiency and confidence. By doodling, sketching, and drawing, not by taking copious notes, I was able to stay on top of my classes and learn quite a bit about language and literature. In other words, students who may not fit the usual good writer mold can be actively involved in an *invention* process, a *development* process, and extensive *revision* processes.

As Golden (1986) observes, "An analogy [can] be made between the genesis of a painting and the creation of a written text. No doubt the artist's use of shapes, the musician's use of notes, and the writer's use of words are distinct. . . . Making allowances for the different symbol systems involved, composition is a concept commonly used in the visual arts and writing. The term signifies the similarities that abound between composing in both arts, especially if we consider not the artistic artifacts but the process by which the image emerges on the canvas or the words appear on the page" (60).

This raises a final important point: *writing derives from vision*. Current cognitive research is establishing links between sight and language (Gutin 1996), but the link already manifests itself intuitively in the language we use daily. We see the point; we speak in metaphors; we acknowledge insight. Ignoring the connections between the visual and verbal would mean ignoring years of research that emphasize their interdependencies in the learning process. It would also mean ignoring a rich pedagogical resource for writing and literature classrooms.

Acknowledging the connections between visual and verbal literacy is the first step. Enacting that understanding in the classroom follows logically, yet, as we know from our own experiences in making this perceptual transition, engaging a process of change is not easy. If nothing else, it requires talents we aren't always completely certain we have. Our hope, however, is that you can begin to visualize the type of visual-verbal integration presented in the following pages, and incorporate similar activities into your own classroom instruction. We know the results will be rewarding.

Response

Pamela B. Childers

In speaking for the three of us, Eric clearly states our belief "that the linkages that connect the composing processes they [visual artists] manipulate to create their work seem absurdly obvious." We learn this connection anew each time we work with another visual artist. And because we in the world of teaching writing have stolen so many of their ideas—most obviously portfolios—why shouldn't we look further to see writing in the context of a visual world?

The close relationship between the composing process in writing and the composing process in art is one of our key points. I remember the first time I saw the drafts of Degas' horse sketches at the National Gallery in Washington, D.C. As an English teacher, my initial reaction was, *Now I can explain the role of revision in writing by using visual examples.* Some of the sketches clearly had minuscule variations; others demonstrated large changes in perspective. When I saw the final draft, I knew this visual metaphor would work in the classroom. No one had marked the sketches with circled mistakes; the changes were the artist's, the results of *seeing* the composition critically in a different way. This action correlates directly with what we want our students to do in revising their writing: to examine their ideas critically and modify the text to reflect that new way of *seeing*.

If we are going to explore the connections between visual and verbal learning, we must overcome the fear of inadequacy that Eric describes so well. When we are put in the position of using an unfamiliar medium, we resemble our colleagues in other disciplines when they are asked to teach writing. We fear that since we are not masters of the visual arts or visual artists, we shouldn't be using the visual arts in teaching writing.

By taking this risk, however, we model learning and writing as colearners with our students. If we approach writing as our students do, through discovery, perhaps we will likewise gain a better understanding of this shared experience. It will also open a new kind of dialogue between us. I still remember with delight not knowing what kind of bizarre still life awaited us in the art studio until I arrived with my class to write (see Chapter 5). If I had stopped by the art classroom to look at the design before class, I could not have reacted genuinely to this new visual experience, and the poem that resulted would not have reflected my spontaneous response to my visual surroundings. The students were amazed at what the still life triggered in them, and the discussion that followed demonstrated critical thinking on a level that required active participation from the beginning.

Eric's Activity

The added bonus of Eric's workshop activity is that it gives us a better understanding of the position we put our colleagues in when we ask them to use writing in teaching their disciplines. Like Eric, I have found that teachers in other disciplines are eager to try visual techniques, and that gets me in the door much faster than if I suggest writing across the curriculum first. In "drawing" a student, the focus is on the student, not on creating a work of art. It is an exercise in creating metaphors for our writing, in trying to describe, and *picture* a person through a medium other than words. My drawing is the one Eric labeled "the norm." As "visually challenged" as I may be, I have to admit I did not respond in any of the ways Eric found common. I've come to accept my limitations as an artist, and in leading numerous writing workshops I have learned the value of risk taking. However, these reactions ("I've never been good at drawing," "I don't know what you want") are the very ones our students give in class when we ask them to write. This activity makes participants sensitive to their own students' experience. It puts them in the role of a learner who does not know the answer or the "secret formula" the teacher knows. The last time I did this activity with a group of secondary English teachers, we all found it difficult to create the drawing without using words. This frustration of not having a "language" with which to communicate surprised us all.

I remember many years ago sharing a writing experience with poet Donald Hall. A group of us exchanged first drafts for feedback, as did Mr. Hall. When it came time to respond to his draft, we all darted around the issue trying to say something vague and complimentary about the piece. Finally, he confided that his writing is mediocre at best until it goes through many drafts. That experience taught us that not all writers use the same process.

Eric's workshop activity also reinforces the idea that there may not be one *right* answer. For many participants this is a surprise or something they have long forgotten. The anxiety associated with committing something to paper, whether in writing or in "pictures" that others may see, becomes concrete—we cannot deny what we have created. Our spoken words can be denied, explained, even mumbled! Ownership of marks on a piece of paper is harder to sidestep.

Learning Styles

Eric also mentions how important students' learning styles and personality profiles may be in their success or failure in our educational systems. His own experience in using visual note taking in school, and the teacher's reaction, is not unique. As he reminds us, we frequently see our writing classes as totally verbal. For this reason especially, I believe a visual environment is essential in a writing center. In the Caldwell Writing Center at the McCallie School, for instance, whether they are working at computers or large tables, students are surrounded by "visuals." Two sides of the center have large windows framing the hallway on one side and a view from Missionary Ridge of Chattanooga and its distant mountains on the other. On any given day, spectacular skies, rainbows, even the practice flights of the Blue Angels, will stop us from writing or inspire writing. The other two walls are covered with giant art posters from the Geraldine R. Dodge Poetry Festivals, prints of original landscapes, purchased photographs of world-famous mountains or sights I have captured, and cartoons that stimulate students' imaginations.

Eric's doodled symbols were his verbal cues to the words, ideas, and relationships he had learned in class that day. Many artists, naturalists, scientists, photographers, journalists, and writers of all sorts use field journals or notebooks that include sketches and words. An artist friend visited the Provence region of France, where Vincent van Gogh lived and worked. Her intent was to see what he had seen and create her own watercolor interpretations for her journal. In looking through the pages of her journal, I was more fascinated by the mixture of art and words than by her watercolor landscapes, because I realized that she had substituted visual symbols for the words she did not know in French. One delightful double page spread recorded a special lunch she had attended one sunny day. She had drawn pictures of each food amid the words she jotted to describe the host and hostess, the sequence of courses, what was said, and so on. By the time I had read to dessert under a willow tree and eyed the painted strawberries, I was salivating. She created the entire mood by combining the visual (in translucent watercolors) and the verbal (in black ink).

Eric's discussion of learning styles touches on an issue many secondary educators have been dealing with for years. A variety of learning styles inventories (Dunn and Dunn 1978; Fleming and Mills 1992), including the NASSP Learning Style Profile (1986), are now available as computer software that can be easily scored and evaluated. Boarding schools and colleges have been using them to pair dormitory roommates according to best study times, the effect of light and sound on reading, and sleeping requirements, for example. Classroom teachers and parents of secondary students have attended inservice programs so that they can approach learning through as many teaching styles as possible. Teachers are encouraged to give directions orally, to write them on the board or hand out copies, and even to offer alternative assignments when necessary. Visually impaired students qualify for books on tape, dyslexic and dysgraphic students are given extra time to read or write responses on tests, and ADD (Attention Deficit Disorder) students frequently get hands-on activities to focus them on their learning. Unfortunately, knowing that these various learning styles may coexist in one classroom does not make the job easier for trained professional educators, but it does make students more aware of how they learn.

Eric's approach puts more responsibility for learning on learners themselves, once they know their dominant learning style. The VARK inventory (Fleming and Mills 1992) seems to lend strong support to the need to integrate visual and verbal writing instruction. If teachers could focus basically on this method of instruction, perhaps this pedagogical shift might ensure improved learning and writing.

Just as Eric has questioned his own teaching of writing in his college-level course, those of us on the secondary level wonder if we can reach the students who are there for reasons other than learning—warmth in winter, meals, a place to store their belongings (a locker), a shower, and people who care whether or not they are alive. I remember many senior skills classes of students and seeing sparks of learning with their writing only when they were given the opportunity to mix the visual and the verbal. One year, I raised enough money from a variety of sources to take the class to see a Broadway musical. Those eighteen-year-olds squirmed in their seats with the excitement of six-year-olds, and they had no trouble finding something to write about the next day.

Another year, before the luxury of videos, individual students viewed Super 8 film loops of historical events and scientific projects.

Many undertook self-motivated research projects based on these short films. One project in particular that fascinated me was on Siamese fighting fish. After viewing the film loop, Harry, a regular sleeper in my English class, decided he would get a red and a blue Siamese fish from the biology lab and bring them to our classroom in a large aquarium, separating the fish until he was ready. We set a class period aside for Harry's experiment. He invited other students and created a scoreboard. Harry had even taped labels for each fish—Pink Pad and Big Blue—to the front of the aquarium. The scoreboard included such items as: two points for forcing the opponent to back up, and three points for raising a dorsal fin. I suggested that we needed a referee to call the fight before either fish was seriously injured. He agreed that I could handle that role as long as I allowed some points to accumulate; there had to be some action for his experiment!

By the time class started and the divider between the two fish was removed, we had double the enrollment in the room and cheering sections for Pink Pad and Big Blue. Harry explained the rules and held chalk in hand ready to record points for each side. The fight was on! In less than ten minutes, I called the fight with Big Blue the victor. Half the students disappeared to whatever class they were skipping, and Harry was writing down his observations and asking his classmates for input. After visits to the biology teacher to get more information on these fish, Harry wrote a paper most seniors would have been proud to claim. The use of the visual with the verbal had done the trick. Of course, there were some rumors that Harry may have been taking some bets on the fight, but we never found any proof of that.

Not surprisingly, I discovered that it wasn't just the visual that fascinated Harry; he had seen lots of movies. He was intrigued by the black-and-white format of authentic historical film. From fish, he next turned to the Scopes Trial, stopping and starting the short Super 8 film loop on frames of William Jennings Bryan and Clarence Darrow. "These were real people, weren't they?" he whispered to me after the third day of viewing. "Yes," I said, "and the trial still has an influence on the way people think." I found him a copy of *Inherit the Wind*, and Harry took off for the library to find everything he could on the Scopes Trial, Bryan, and Darrow. Within a week, Harry had made himself an authority on the topic and written an entire research paper in which he proposed that Bryan did not die of a heart attack: he was murdered. When he presented his paper to the class, he once again used the film loop and stopped it two or three times to try to prove his point. Today I have seen many Harrys getting the same kind of excitement from viewing videos to inspire their research and writing.

Postscript

As learners and as teachers, all of us may have different styles, but sensitivity to the learning styles of others may help us revise our teaching styles or shift our pedagogical paradigms. The three of us are not suggesting that we all teach the same way. Instead, we are stating that as teachers of writing, we must be aware of the role visual elements play in students' learning processes. If we are aware, we can find ways to encourage students' active involvement in their writing.

chapter

2

Postcards: Inside/Out

JOSEPH F. TRIMMER

This Is the Way It Used to Be

My college-level writing students, silent and somber, followed me up the grand staircase, through the massive arch, and into the main gallery of the art museum. They studied the colored maps as I explained the arrangement of the rooms beyond the velvet ropes. And then, in groups of threes and fours, they strolled down the halls, disappearing into the museum for what I presumed would be an adventure in seeing. I trailed along hoping to see what they saw. But I was never fast enough. I lost most of them immediately as they channel surfed their way from one gallery to another. Those that lingered seemed confused. Some were more impressed by the size of the rooms than by the paintings on the walls. Some were more interested in the words on the plaques than in the images in the frames, while still others stared quietly at each painting, and then, unable to decipher the message, drifted on to the next puzzle.

I made my way through the maze, seeing fewer and fewer students, until I got to the gift shop. And there they were, hunting for bargains among the calendars, posters, and postcards that featured the paintings they had just seen. But what was I seeing? The results of a museum culture that enshrined art in spaces that alienated observers? The results of a commercial culture that promoted shopping as the greatest good? Or something more subtle? The results of an information explosion that prompted individuals, overloaded by images and words, to purchase a single token—a postcard that stood for *all that out there* that they could not understand?

This Is What We Did

I decided to play it their way. Instead of taking my writing students to the art museum, I brought the "gift shop" to them. I invited them to sort through a stack of postcards, select one they liked, and then use it for a journal assignment. The first time around, the assignment was fairly simple:

> 1. Free Write: Tape the postcard in your journal and then free write about it. For example, you may want to assume the identity of one of the characters in your painting and write about what you see.

The students began writing and did not stop until the end of class. When I picked up their journals, I noticed that each entry was over seven pages long. When I began reading them, I realized that their sketches explored the relationship between artist, subject, and observer. I could see that I had stumbled onto a powerful prompt, but I could not see how to use it.

By our next meeting, my students had it all figured out. They wanted to read their journal entries to the class. They wanted to exchange entries with each other. They wanted to mix and match entries to enact a dialogue between different paintings. Indeed, they wanted to design a sequence of writing assignments to learn more about their postcards. And so together we began brainstorming, drafting, and revising a sequence of assignments to organize their responses to and their research about the painting on their postcard. The postcard became their icon and the sequence their "search engine," enabling them to explore the web of information inside and outside their little window on the worlds of art and culture.

This is What Kathy Did

One of my students, Kathy Conrow, selected a postcard of Winslow Homer's *The Blue Boy* (1873) [see cover] and began converting her free write into several creative responses to the painting:

> 2. Narrate: Use some of the information you discovered in your free write to compose a coherent narrative about your character. Tell us your story.

> Phinny and I have been brothers all our lives. He's two years older than I am, but he still lets me go just about everywhere with him.

Some mornings he goes out to the field where the cows graze and just sits there for hours, watching and thinking. I'm not sure what he thinks about or why he has to sit in the field to do it, but I go with him and wait. One day while we were sitting in the sun, stripping pieces of grass, and studying the cows, Phinny told me a story about the ship anchored down in the harbor.

3. Observe: Describe the person (or persons) who are looking at you as you hang on the wall. What are they looking at? What are they thinking about as they look at you? How have these observers changed over the years? How does it feel to be *unobserved*?

I hate Mondays. The museum is always closed. The lights are dimmed, the doors are locked and there's a heavy silence in the halls. No slamming doors, no footsteps, no hushed voices arguing about the meaning of art or whether it's time for lunch. It's just us, hanging in the darkness. Some don't mind this time alone, a break from pointing fingers and quizzical stares. But I miss the people. I like to eavesdrop when they talk about what they think we see at the bottom of the hill. I like to watch them squint as they move closer to look at my feet or the birds in the sky.

4. Respond: Write a monologue about your creation. Who painted you? How did you decide on how you would pose? How long, and how often did you have to pose? What did the painter's face look like as he studied you from behind the canvas? When were you allowed to see yourself? What do you think about your portrait?

I was surprised when I saw Mr. Homer trudging up the hill with his wooden case and thick tablet. I'd seen him by the boatyards earlier in the week when he sketched Billy and his friend as they stared at the boats. But why did he want to make a picture in the middle of a field? There were no tall ships or old docks. Just Phinny, me, and the cows. Mr. Homer said he'd like to paint us anyway, if we didn't mind, and started unpacking his brushes and examining his pencils. Once he arranged his materials, he arranged us. He wanted one of us to sit and the other to stand. We started to argue about who would sit, but when Mr. Homer said he would paint the face of the standing boy, I let Phinny have a seat. The sun was hot on the back of my neck, but there was a slight breeze from the harbor below.

  Mr. Homer worked fairly fast, sketching first with his pencil, then dipping his brush into a puddle of colored water, and dashing it on to the paper. He was so involved in his work, he barely noticed when I looked at him over my shoulder. Occasionally he would lean back to study the painting, then he would scowl at some little section of the paper, and reach out to add one or two quick dashes.

  Things were going fine until my hat blew off. Phinny's stayed on all right, but mine kept blowing off. Every time I had to retrieve it, Mr. Homer had to stop painting. About the third time, Mr. Homer said he'd go get it and I should just stay. So he grabbed it and put it back on my head, twisting it around like he was trying to screw it on. But even that didn't work. The wind slipped under the brim and flipped it behind me. Finally Mr. Homer stopped another boy who was walking through the field and asked him to stand a couple of feet behind me to capture my hat if it blew off. This worked for a while. But when Mr. Homer applied one or two dashes near the top of his drawing, he took my hat, wrapped it in his jacket, and laid it beside his case until he was through for the day.

5. Collaborate: Compose a dialogue with a person in a painting that hangs next to you or on the opposite wall. What do the two of you have to say to each other after all these years? Do you admire, annoy, or avoid one another? What do the people who come and go have to say about the two of you?

The other day when things were slow, and the only people in the room were the ones in grey jackets, I decided to see how the shad-fishermen were doing. They hung right below me and I liked talking to them since I am from Gloucester, Massachusetts, and they are from Gloucester, New Jersey. They remind me of the fishermen I see in the boatyards down by the harbor.

    The man kneeling at the water's edge is the one I talk to most.

    "How are things down there in the fishing business today?"

    "About the same. Weather looks good again, but we're still having trouble with this one net." They were always having trouble with that one net.

    "Do you think you're going to get out today?"

    "We keep hoping, but it's starting to look doubtful." It had been years since they had been out on the river, and I am surprised that they haven't given up by now. But somehow, each morning, they manage to start with renewed enthusiasm.

    "I wish I could leave this field and help you. I've watched the fishermen down in the harbor for years. I might be able to fix that net." [Thomas Eakins, *Shad Fishing at Gloucester-on-the-Delaware*, 1881] (Figure 2–1)

The first five assignments invite students to play with the worlds inside their postcard and with the worlds outside, where they circulate. Their storytelling does not have to be accurate because its purpose is to encourage their identification with their painting, to help them imagine the conditions that attended its creation and have accompanied its exhibition. But inevitably, students start to investigate the clues on the back of their postcard. They want to know something about the painter, when he painted this particular painting, who the people were who posed for him, what was significant about the place

Figure 2–1

Thomas Eakins, *Shad Fishing at Gloucester-on-the-Delaware* (1881) [see p. iv for credit line]

they posed, why he selected a particular painting technique, and how this painting figures in his life and the history of painting.

Kathy's creative speculations about Homer's *The Blue Boy* prompted her to read several biographies. She discovered that 1873 was a turning point in Homer's career as he spent the summer in Gloucester, Massachusetts, painting watercolors of the local children. She used some of this information to enrich her creative writing, but the more she read, the more she wanted to conduct a formal investigation of the painting.

To conduct such an investigation, however, Kathy had to measure her imaginative speculations against the evidence of scholarship. She also had to modulate the subjective tone of her creative voice to the more objective tone of the critical voice. And finally, as she practiced with this new voice, she had to amplify and verify it by quoting, paraphrasing, and documenting the authoritative voices she discovered in her research.

6. Investigate: Read some biographies about the artist who painted you. Who are you? What is your relationship to the artist? When did he paint you? What events prompted him to paint you? What special techniques did he use to capture your image? How do you compare to other portraits he painted?

Scattered flecks of gauche grasses and field flowers, the clean white-paper shirts of meditative children, the lifted-out lights of early summer skies—these are some of the details of sun-drenched days in Gloucester, Massachusetts, that Winslow Homer captured in his first finished watercolor paintings. Before his visit to the old fishing town, Homer's watercolors might be "described as colored wash drawings" (Cooper, 20). But his experiments in the summer of 1873 enabled him to use the medium in a new and innovative way, establishing him, eventually, as "its greatest master in the history of American art" (Cikovsky, 53).

Homer's decision to delve into this transparent medium remains mysterious. His mother was an accomplished watercolorist (Cikovsky, 54), so he was aware of the medium, but he was almost thirty-eight years old before he decided to work with it himself. Nicolai Cikovsky suggests that Homer may have been influenced by the international watercolor exhibition held in New York earlier in the year (54). The exhibition demonstrated that watercolor could be used to create more than simple sketches and delicate decorations; and Homer "surely perceived that watercolors, which could be made more quickly and in greater abundance than oil paintings, and sold more cheaply, could be a more reliable source of income" (54).

The characteristics of watercolor pigments and the qualities of his subject matter also played a part in Homer's decision. Every paint medium has unique properties that cause it to behave in certain ways and allow it to be manipulated to achieve different effects. Watercolor, with its translucent qualities and capacities for capturing brilliant light, made it perfectly suited for the bright airiness of the Gloucester summer shore. The changing moments of shadow and reflection could be captured in broad washes, lifted-out lights and sparkling white paper; and the warm, glowing colors of sun-lit sand, fields, water, and sky could be achieved with fast drying layers of transparent wash (Wilmerding, 90).

The portability of watercolor also made it ideal for Homer's subject and setting. There was no cumbersome easel, bulky canvas, or cans of turpentine to haul around. As he combed the beaches of Gloucester for subjects or climbed the grassy slope where he made *The Blue Boy*, he needed only pigment, paper, brush and water, all of which could be carried with little trouble from one summer scene to the next. Helen A. Cooper suggests such portability "established what would be . . . Homer's lifelong pattern in watercolor: concentrating on a particular time on a single theme suggested by a particular locale" (24–25).

7. Analyze: Read some art criticism about yourself. What are some of the distinctive features of your image that art lovers have admired over the years? What are the particular features of your portrait that have created the most debate among critics?

Kathy elected to skip assignment 7 because she dealt with much of this information in her treatment of assignment 6. When she studied 8, she considered several topics: "Homer and His Contemporaries," "American Landscape Painting," and "The Watercolor Movement." She also considered looking at the problem of influence: the fresh air school, Japanese painting, and the emerging school of impressionism have all been cited as possible influences on the development of Homer's style. But most art historians characterize Homer as a solitary traveler, discovering his own way without the aid of instruction or influence. What finally interested Kathy about her postcard was its title, *The Blue Boy*. She remembered another painting with the same title painted by a different painter in a different style. The possibilities for a provocative comparison seemed promising.

8. Evaluate: Read some history about other artists who painted during the time you were painted *or* who painted figures like you in other times. How do art historians compare you to your contemporaries? How do they compare you to similar figures painted in other times?

The Blue Boy is a barefoot child wearing a straw hat. He is also a wealthy young man in blue satin holding a plumed hat. He is standing on a hill against a pale blue sky and on another hill with brown clouds at his back. He is ordinary and aristocratic; paired and alone; in profile and staring defiantly at the viewer.

How can these contrasting descriptions characterize one painting? The reason is simple—there are two paintings entitled *The Blue Boy*, two separate images created in different times by different artists: Winslow Homer's light-filled watercolor of a boy in a straw hat (1873), and Thomas Gainsborough's darker portrait of an elegantly dressed young man (1770).

These "Blue Boy" paintings have few similarities beyond their shared name. A handful of elemental details, such as a diagonally moving landscape, shoots of yellow grass scattered on the hill, and the vague suggestion of trees in the distance, can be seen in both, but the duplication of these points is most likely coincidental. The artists' reasons for including them in their works, however, may have been the same. The diagonal, for example, is a strong element in any composition. It adds drama and carries the eye across the landscape (Cormack, 100). The shoots of grass add detail and definition, and the vague tree forms build distance, perspective, and a deeper sense of space.

But the artists executed these details in completely different settings and media. Homer worked outdoors, painting the ordinary children in a Massachusetts fishing town—elements well-suited to the portability and spontaneous nature of the liquid medium (Cooper, 24). Indeed, he was experimenting with watercolor just as it had begun "to attract the serious and widespread interest of professional American artists, their critics and their patrons"(Cikovsky, 54).

Gainsborough, on the other hand, worked in a studio, painting lavish portraits of aristocrats from the grand houses of Bath, England (Waterhouse, 19–22). These people expected to be depicted in all their glory, their "virtue in this world . . . rewarded by [the trappings of] social and financial success" (Berger, 103). Gainsborough was working in the established tradition of his time when oil was considered the only medium appropriate for aristocratic subjects.

Such details call attention to the difference between the identity of the two Blue Boys. Homer's boy was just one of the many vague-featured children he painted in profile during his summer in Gloucester (Wilmerding, 92). But Gainsborough's young man identifies himself by staring directly at the viewer, allowing himself to be named. He was Jonathan Buttall, son of a wealthy Soho ironmonger and a close friend of the artist. But according to art historian Malcolm Cormack, "X-rays have revealed that the portrait was painted on a discarded canvas, so that it may well have been done for pleasure instead of on commission" (100). Nevertheless, Gainsborough placed his friend in a grand landscape and posed him, hand on hip, attired in a vibrant blue suit, holding a large feathered hat.

These comparisons suggest other differences between the two paintings. Homer's anonymous boy looks away from the viewer, but he seems accessible. The light of the sky, the warmth of the field, the company of a friend, as well as paired cows and birds, and the casual summer clothing welcome the viewer into his familiar, comfortable world. Gainsborough's boy (Jonathan Buttall) stares boldly at the viewer, but he seems remote. The brown sky, the desolate hill, and his fancy costume warn the viewer that his world is formidable and exclusive.

Kathy invested so much time writing about her postcard that she began to see it as *hers*. When she studied assignment 9, she decided to explore the problem of ownership. She purchased a museum catalogue and began sorting out the details listed under *provenance*—the museum's method for recording the history of who has owned a work of art. Next, she requested permission to study in the museum's archives and to obtain the file on *The Blue Boy*. She spent several days reading old letters, bills of sale, and catalogue descriptions. She finally visited Elisabeth Ball's home—now an environmental center called Oakhurst Gardens—to find the bedroom where *The Blue Boy* hung for over forty years until it was moved to the museum. Her research enabled her to trace the curatorial history of the painting and speculate about her curious attachment to her postcard.

9. Document: Trace your curatorial history. Who has owned you? Why did they buy you? Where did they hang you? Why did they sell you? What is the highest price anybody has paid for you? Who paid it—a private collector? a museum? Where can we find you now? What kind of company do you keep? What other paintings hang in your room? Where did they come from?

Since *The Blue Boy* was created in 1873 many people have called it "my painting." On that day in June, the boys on the hill may have been the first to call it theirs—seeing the finished piece, recognizing themselves in the washes, sensing that they would always be part of the painting and its history. Of course, their claims had nothing to do with actual possession. That claim was Winslow Homer's. He composed the scene, created the painting, and claimed it as "my painting" when he signed his name in blue in the lower left corner.

It was also his hand, however, that left the inscription "to M.F." next to his name, indicating that he wished to share his painting with another. Whether this mark was intended as a dedication or to indicate a future gift is unclear, but if we assume M.F. was Mattie French Homer, Winslow's sister-in-law, then the inscription would eventually come to mean both.

In 1910, when Winslow Homer died, Mattie and her husband, Charles Savage Homer, Jr., were the next to call *The Blue Boy* "my painting." Winslow lived near Charles and Mattie, especially during their summers at Prout's Neck in Maine, and he had a special admiration for his sister-in-law. He would take her bouquets each day from the garden he kept by his studio, and he would write to her, and his brother, regularly when they were away (Graham, 30).

Mattie developed a great appreciation for Homer's work and tried to keep others interested in it after Homer, and then her husband, died. She opened his studio to visitors and took flowers there often, possibly repaying his gifts to her (Graham, 31). According to her niece, Louise Homer Graham, Mattie also kept Winslow's works in her home in West Townsend, Massachusetts, and the family place at Prout's Neck. *The Blue Boy* was most likely one of these paintings, and as Mattie passed it each day she could say that's "my painting." It became hers officially in 1910, but if the dedication "M.F." was meant for her, then she had always possessed part of it.

When Mattie died in 1937, another member of the Homer family was able to call *The Blue Boy* "my painting." Mrs. Arthur P. Homer (Anna), Winslow's niece-in-law, lived next door to Mattie when she was in West Townsend. It's likely that Anna occasionally saw the impressive collection that covered Mattie's walls, and she may have commented on *The Blue Boy* at some point. But whether or not she had a previous affection for the painting, it became hers in 1937, and she was able to call it "my painting" for about four years.

In February 1941 it was passed on again and, for the first time, to someone outside the Homer family. It went to William Macbeth,

Inc., an art dealer in New York City. In the hands of a dealer, "my painting" took on a new meaning. Although the painting was still appreciated for its artistic elements, it was appreciated even more for its economic possibilities. These concerns are expressed in letters from Robert McIntyre, a representative of William Macbeth, Inc., to Elisabeth Ball (the future owner of *The Blue Boy*) and her mother, Mrs. Frances Ball. In one of these letters, McIntyre wrote, "In all cases of art objects the thing to consider is estate taxes" (3 June 1955). And in another, he explains his personal feelings about the collection of "expensive pictures" saying, "In my own case, I do know that even if I could afford to own expensive pictures, I should be afraid to die possessed of them. What the 'wolves' would do to my widow would be just too horrible to think about!" (10 May 1955).

These letters follow McIntyre's advice to Miss Ball to sell a few of her more expensive paintings, a sale he would have been glad to arrange. His job was to *move* paintings—to relieve some people of art and to help others acquire it. To the employees of William Macbeth, Inc., "my painting," in connection with *The Blue Boy*, meant "mine briefly, mine to move, mine to sell." And sell it they did, just over a year after they received it.

On May 8, 1942, Elisabeth Ball found *The Blue Boy* in their gallery in New York. She had been looking for another Homer watercolor ever since she had read about the famous painter in Lois Homer Graham's article, "An Intimate Glimpse of Winslow Homer's Art," in the May 1936 issue of *Vassar Journal of Undergraduate Studies*. She had purchased her first Homer, *Rendezvous*, in 1936 on a New York "shopping" excursion (Fraser, 95). On another of these excursions, she found *The Blue Boy*, purchased it for $1,500, marked down from its original price of $1,800, and took it back to Oakhurst, her lifelong home in Muncie, Indiana, where it became "my painting."

According to a list made in her own hand, Elisabeth Ball hung *The Blue Boy* in "My Bedroom," along with a T. C. Steele oil painting of peonies, a pair of pastel portraits by T. W. Dewing, and at least two other watercolors—one entitled *Shepherd and Sheep* signed A. Mauve, and the other of an Indian village with palm trees by L. C. Maurice Gordon. At one point, it was also joined by another Winslow Homer watercolor called *The Ranger, Adirondacks*, which was painted in 1892 and acquired by Elisabeth not long after she purchased *The Blue Boy*.

In 1955, when Robert McIntyre encouraged Elizabeth to sell some of her "more expensive pictures," he mentioned Homer's *The Blue Boy*, as well as Thomas Eakins' *Shad Fishing at Gloucester on the Delaware*, saying he thought they would "fare very well at this time" (10 May 1955). Fortunately, Elisabeth was not persuaded by this advice and kept the paintings until her death in April 1982. At that time the paintings were passed, along with many other pieces of her collection, to the George and Frances Ball Foundation, Muncie, Indiana. In January 1984, they were exhibited in the Elisabeth Ball

Collection of the Ball State University Museum of Art and were finally given to the museum in 1996.

The Blue Boy still hangs on the second floor of the museum. Beneath it hangs Eakins' work mentioned in McIntyre's letter. Every
day many people stroll up to the painting, stop and look. Like Mattie and Elisabeth, many of these people like to think of it as "my
painting."

I've become one of those people. Digging into its history, its
artist, and its owners, I feel like I've developed my own special claim
on The Blue Boy. Like the boys on the hill, mine has nothing to do
with real possession. But whenever I see that watercolor—on the
wall of the museum, on the page of a book, or the face of a postcard,
I say that's "my painting."

When Kathy finished her curatorial history, she had one more
writing assignment to consider. She also had to consider the significance of the Winslow Homer Exhibition (1996) that had recently
opened at the National Gallery in Washington, D.C., without The Blue
Boy. She confessed she was ambivalent: "I feel rejected. If people studied the cultural history of the time, or had any aesthetic sensibilities,
they would appreciate the special qualities of The Blue Boy. On the
other hand, I feel relieved. The Blue Boy won't be traveling from museum to museum—like a homeless painting. It belongs on the second
floor of the art museum. Instead of writing assignment 10, I think I'll
go see "my painting."

> 10. Argue: Working from the information you have gathered about
> yourself, construct one of the following arguments:
>   a. You are the best portrait your artist ever painted.
>   b. You are the most representative/innovative portrait painted
>   in your time.
>   c. You cannot be appreciated unless someone studies the cul-
>   tural history of your time.
>   d. You can be fully appreciated by anyone in any time because
>   of your timeless beauty.

This Is the Way It Is Now

I follow my writing students up the grand staircase, through the massive arch, and into the main gallery of the art museum. I study the
colored map as they explain the sequence of presentations they plan
to give in the rooms beyond the velvet ropes. And then we stroll
down the halls, as a class, for a true adventure in seeing.

We stop in a gallery to hear a student read a creative response or
a critical analysis of his or her painting. Often these readings create

new conversations among the reader and the students whose paintings hang on other walls in the gallery or in other galleries in the museum. Sometimes these conversations focus on the differences between rooms, frames, and plaques. Sometimes they focus on differences of subject and technique. And sometimes they focus on the unexpected connections between paintings, painters, or moments in cultural history.

I am no longer the teacher. My students have become sophisticated consumers, explaining to me and each other the significance of "their painting." And although they develop a strong attachment to their postcard, they are interested in the others. So eventually, all of us are back in the gift shop. Like Robert McIntyre, we can't "afford to own expensive pictures," but we can afford to collect postcards and to study the many worlds—inside and out—they enable us to see.

Works Cited

Berger, John. 1972. *Ways of Seeing.* London: BBC.

Cikovsky, Nicolai, Jr. 1990. *Winslow Homer.* New York: Abrams.

Cooper, Helen A. 1986. *Winslow Homer Watercolors.* New Haven: Yale University Press.

Cormack, Malcolm. 1991. *The Paintings of Thomas Gainsborough.* Cambridge: Cambridge University Press.

———. Letter to Elisabeth Ball. 10 May 1955. Elisabeth Ball Collection Documents, Volume II. Muncie, IN: Ball State University Museum of Art.

Fraser, Marie. 1984. "The Elisabeth Ball Art Collection." *Oakhurst Poems and Other Scripts of Elisabeth Ball,* edited by Hope Barns, 95–99. Catalogue. Ball State University, Muncie, IN.

Graham, Louise Homer. "The Homers and Prout's Neck." In *Winslow Homer in the 1890's: Prout's Neck Observed* 25–33. New York: Hudson.

———. "An Intimate Glimpse of Winslow Homer's Art." 1936. *Vassar Journal of Undergraduate Studies* 10 (May): 2–3.

McIntyre, Robert. 1955. Letter to Mrs. Frances Ball. 3 June. Elisabeth Ball Collection. Waterhouse, Ellis. 1958. *Gainsborough.* London: Hulton.

Wilmerding, John. 1972. *Winslow Homer.* New York: Praeger.

Response

JOAN A. MULLIN

Joe Trimmer's chapter causes multidisciplinary explosions in the Writing Across the Curriculum (WAC) part of my brain. That's about as visual a response to the chapter as I can give: from the central idea of bringing artifacts from the museum to the classroom, I, like the students, imagine pathways of learning in all directions. What is more,

- *The project is adaptable to any area of the country.* Every community has some local museum or historical society, is near to such resources, or can draw on the resources from state boards of commerce and tourism. Botanical societies, entomology collections, art books, even local galleries could be adapted for use as a research project that students could *own*.

- *When students become the class expert on a subject, motivation runs high.* Students are so often the subjects in class: subjected to texts, subjected to our knowledge; subjected to our ways of thinking about the world. By giving them the position of expert, they not only gain self-confidence as researchers and writers, but they begin to understand the concept of lifelong learning—they see us learn from them. The other side of their being in this expert position is that students more easily accept evaluation. The questions I may raise seem not "correctional" but sincere attempts to understand what students are saying; I become an honest audience, one that doesn't have a preconceived answer. Students readily respond with either more information or more research when I ask questions like "How did that happen?" "I don't understand the connection between the art and the point you are making." "Can you give me more examples of this, or is this a single incident in the artist's creative life?" They want to explain.

- *These exercises ease students into becoming research experts—tasks most of us have difficulty designing.* How many techniques have you developed over the years to motivate student interest in research projects? How many have, nonetheless, produced bored students about halfway through? Even when they choose their subject, even when we help them narrow the topic, students often seem to lose interest in it and thus don't benefit from the experience as much as they could. By using a visual anchor that still provides plenty of subject options, this project teaches students about the wealth of perspectives one can take on any research project: a painting holds many points of view; many pieces of the canvas can be studied; there are assumptions that guided its creation; there are cultural conditions that affected its production. One of the elements in developing critical thinking skills is the ability to see from several points of view, to choose one, to investigate a subject's many sides.

- *The project is inexpensive:* most school budgets would agree to pitch in for postcards. However, you could also direct students to museum stores and ask them to buy a card of their own choosing. Those of us with limited or shrinking budgets know that sometimes simple requests are denied. Students with limited or shrinking budgets would appreciate buying a postcard rather than a generic text on how to do research.

For all of these reasons, I am most excited about how Trimmer's ideas translate into useful projects for faculty across the disciplines or areas.

Disciplinary Variations

English

Trimmer made me think about connecting the pieces of literature students study with the art being produced at that time. Some of us have taught interdisciplinary humanities courses of this nature, but usually the two are taught to students by experts (teachers), or one field augments the other. What if students' obligation in a literature class was to read the text and then enlarge their understanding of it from the perspective of their artist's work? Using the prompts Trimmer suggests or others, course work outside of class would consist of writing about the artwork. Class discussion would center on the literary piece, but with a difference: the usual analysis of character, plot, symbolism, and other typical approaches with roots in the New Criticism of the 1940s would be augmented by the social construction, postmodern, deconstructive, new historical perspectives that students would be (unknowingly) bringing into play with their examinations of the artworks.

For example, most of us know of the relationships between the visual and literary movements of the nineteenth-century American Romanticists. The type of landscape painting of that century, in fact the very landscapes artists painted, appear in many of the canonical works by authors like Longfellow, Hawthorne, Melville, and Thoreau, which are still taught. Students could investigate a painting, its origin, its place in the art of the time, its artist, its relationship to the art that now surrounds it in the museum in which it hangs, and begin to draw relationships and correspondences to the literature discussed in class. Students would enlarge the class's knowledge of the era but would also be able to contribute specific insights to the work of literature as given shape by their outside "art" readings and writing.

Noncanonical authors, specifically those who wrote some of the slave narratives that have been recovered, are equally supported by their absence from the visual representations of the time and by their covert presence in some of the paintings, or by the folk art that continued to thrive and now appears in many museums. In these cases, historical societies and houses in the National Registry may especially prove fertile visual grounds for student postcards and pictures.

History/Art History

In ways similar to those I've suggested for English, history students could create a historical/cultural moment from postcards of artworks. In addition, collections of postcards sent from the front in World War I are available (I have some that I found at a garage sale); there are postcards of Civil War battlefields; and reproductions of postcards from World's Fairs or the Columbian Exposition in Chicago can be bought. Students in history courses could also become the expert voices on particular parts of the period being studied. A presentation by students at the end of the course would be an enlargement of what was contained in the textbook or primary resources used for the course.

Another possibility in a history course is to have students literally recreate a postcard chosen by the class to represent the period. A take-off on the design course outlined by Richard Putney in this collection, this project would ask that students each choose a section of the postcard to investigate: create dialogues with other sections of the card (or other cards if more than one is used in the class), investigate the assumptions behind the photograph (such as, why were people posed this way, why was this angle used, why is the flag included in this shot?), write about the people who are not in the photograph/postcard. Thus, a picture from the Columbian exhibition might be broken into investigative sections. Some students would *represent* and write about the buildings, architects, countries, and politics that created them. Another group might look at how Chicago affected and was affected by the Exposition: Why was it built on the South side? What new construction, materials, and building techniques made it possible to build on this seemingly impossible site? Why was Chicago the site of the exhibition in the first place? Who designed the main buildings, and what would a conversation with other architects in the city have sounded like? What were the politics behind the construction, placement, and eventual destruction of some of the buildings? What remains standing? Why?

While a modern history or urban history course might not center entirely on Chicago, students would learn that questions like these, about a major historical event at a pivotal point in history, grow out of the past and have ramifications for what comes after. Students' work would continually inform and shape the discussion of events.

Final projects could consist of students connecting their group's work to the entire period of history covered during that course— and/or to each other's projects. Activities could also include visual representations: what the site might look like today had it been developed; what the site actually looked like then; what the interior of a single building looked like; what was important about sample materials, construction, or architectural innovations that the building introduced; whether it stimulated a movement in other urban areas or historical periods. Whichever way the course was designed, students would be experiencing the interconnectedness and importance of history. They would be learning why historical data is worth preserving, and how our reading of the past affects (and effects) the present.

A third possibility, one that translates to English as well, is to have students collect their investigations, stimulated by their responsive writings as outlined by Trimmer, into their own history books. The shape, accompanying teaching materials and, of course, the decisions about what to include and what to leave out, would be firsthand lessons in how history is created, thought about, argued. Participating in the creation of a history book would make students more careful and critical readers of facts.

Science

Throughout art, there are depictions of scientific and medical concepts. We have abandoned many of these concepts and materials, yet some still hold sway in popular culture. In a recent science workshop, a presenter asked participants how many of us believed in the theory of relativity. Many raised their hands. The workshop leader then proceeded to debunk our long-held belief in that truth and in many scientific paradigms that we continued to hold (some of which, he pointed out, made us think like our seventeenth-century counterparts!).

I am not suggesting that a science or biology class turn into a writing class at the expense of content. But there are good reasons to think about alternative pedagogy, especially in the high school and in general education or lab courses. According to Sheila Tobias, many students don't learn science because the way science is traditionally taught is geared to those students who learn particularly well in that way (Eric deals further with the issue of learning styles in Chapter 8). These students would learn science with or without the class—and with or without the teacher in many cases. But students who are not oriented toward that factual, hierarchical way of thinking learn best when they can see larger patterns first, relate one concept to another, and write through to understanding. These students would probably benefit from examining a painting and the motivation behind the painting, capturing a breakthrough moment, when, for example, Alexander Graham Bell's invention worked, or the painting of David's *Portrait of Lavoisier* wherein the glass-domed surface complete with chemist's tools points to his discovery of oxygen, or the depiction of alchemical tools on the monk's table, or of the nineteenth-century doctor watching over a woman dying from childbirth.

The significant scientific and medical concepts reflected in those moments affect how we still think about electricity, communication, scientists, doctors, and midwives. These, in turn, affect how we learn about electricity, how we engineer communication tools, how we choose to hypothesize and test those hypotheses, how we establish safe practices for testing drugs, how birthing practices relate to or contradict what we know about the physical process of giving birth. The investigation of biological concepts during critical points in history or how those concepts were overturned is often represented in art—and often available via postcards. In addition to the usual science or lab reports, students could present the relationship of their visual research findings to the class material.

Social Science

Investigating the picture postcards of a cultural moment applies equally to social studies. Rarely does a painting or any artwork involving people, land usage, or monuments not suggest the social movement that created it. I think of the paintings of labor riots, speechifiers of the nineteenth century, depictions of coal miners' conditions, or the art of the sixties that defined and defied a nation. Museums and historical societies likewise present visual snapshots of grassroots groups, immigrants, ethnic cultures, gender gaps.

Political scientists could use some of the same artwork for different purposes by creating different prompts for students, or by simply using similar prompts but asking students to relate the whole to the politics they are studying. For example, students could investigate the many political symbols in David Gilmore Blythe's *The Higher Law, 1861*. In this painting, two white men are confronting each other with daggers. On one side the Southern slave holder is also holding a paper claiming "Our Rights" and he has chained behind him a slave. On the other side an Abolitionist is holding a book called *Higher Law* and the African American watching the quarrel behind him is also picking his pocket. In between the two lies a blood-smeared figure labeled Liberty. Portraits or representations of political moments and presidential moments, as well as the graphic artists' political posters find their way into the museum shops.

Cultural geographers can use some of these same depictions to look at their areas, and all geographers can have students investigate population or location theories in light of representations by various artists and students' critical examination of the pictures before them and the conditions that may have inspired them. Landscape painting, for example, can become a rich resource for considering location, representational validity, and details omitted or present.

All these activities translate easily to psychology classes. Paintings such as Edvard Munch's *The Scream* or Artemesia Gentileschi's version of the biblical story *Judith and Holofernes* provide a wealth of different perspectives that can represent the theories of individual psychologists or send students off on a study of specific human practices. Students could use the postcards to consider the abstract vocabulary and abstract concepts used in discussing the human psyche.

For each of these activities, students could lead their peers through a museum as they present an in-depth psychoanalytical explanation of their painting, or the political dynamics that influenced a particular representation of a president, or the social hysteria underlying a painting of a strike. The museum becomes a resource for critical analysis, for problem solving, and for examining the construction of knowledge (*truth* making).

Et Cetera

In turn, paintings and sculpture can serve as wonderful resources for introducing mathematical concepts. Math teachers can have students study, as many already do, the concepts of proportion, perspective, and point of view, or where the eye falls in the painting. To what end? In the schools, to emphasize the importance of knowing math and its wide-ranging applications. Michelangelo's *David*, for example, could bemoan the oversized, disproportionate hands the artist gave him. But the artist knew what he intended and what that disproportion achieved. The same is true of Donatello's famous *Zuccone*, which, though it originally sat in a high niche on the wall of a church, looked proportional and powerful to the viewers below. (I give these examples because of the unavailability of these pieces of sculpture in this country—let students find their own!)

Real verbal and visual problems already exist in art—why not let students discover them instead of designing Calculus IV tests for them? But what about the final exam? Students must explain their mathematical problem as they tour the museum and describe how they solved it. What place would prompts have in a math class like this? There could be prompts, for example, to discover alternative solutions, to discuss what would happen if the painting could go beyond its frame onto the gallery walls, floors, or ceiling, or where a ball hitting the Ferris wheel in the carnival painting at x miles per hour at an angle of y would end up.

Many of the activities I've suggested can be fine-tuned for vocational arts courses, agriculture courses, or various areas in engineering (chemical, civil, mechanical, and so on): students could write prompts leading to an investigation of the history of a building, of a structural, mechanical, or agricultural technique, of formal gardens or landscaping, of designing a building or a bridge, or of constructing a modern-day mechanical arm from a sketch by Leonardo. And all of these would grow from asking students, as Trimmer did, to examine not just what was apparent to them but what lay behind, around, above, or below, by encouraging students to imagine, create, investigate, and take risks.

Postscript

Trimmer has shown me how to help students discover the tools they need to turn a critical eye on their world. At the same time, he has stepped back as a teacher and handed responsibility for learning over to the students. As we seek to prepare young people for the immense amount of information that is becoming available to them, we must also prepare them to assess what they see, especially when it is computer generated or manipulated. By using art postcards they can hold, examine, live with, and become experts on, we take a giant step in this direction.

Finally, what also occurred to me as I read Trimmer's article is that if I ever have an opportunity to visit Ball State, I would enjoy touring the art gallery with one of his students. Students can play a role in the continuing education all of us need to engage in as teachers, and, if some of their presentations become public, in the education of other faculty, students from across campus, parents, the community, or historical and art societies. What better way to bring the visual into the classroom and to visually bring the classroom into the world?

chapter

3

What's Art Have to Do with It?

PAMELA B. CHILDERS

In the late 1970s I began presenting slides of American art that related to the American literature my English classes were studying. Nothing worked quite so well as linking the transcendentalists with Thomas Cole and the Hudson River School, especially when students saw Asher Durand's painting *Kindred Spirits* showing the poet William Cullen Bryant and the artist Thomas Cole standing on a jutting rock in the Catskill Mountains of New York. The connection between artist and writer was undeniable!

But I wasn't content simply to look at slides of paintings. I wanted more but didn't know what *more* meant. Then, Patrick McCormack, a French teacher at Red Bank Regional High School, in Little Silver, New Jersey, approached me about taking our students on a bus trip to New York City to visit the Metropolitan Museum of Art and the Frick Museum. By the 1980s, Patrick and I were scheduling annual trips for students in junior honors English (American literature) and in the French National Honor Society. I had learned that the American Wing of the Metropolitan offered American literature students a chance to see art associated with the literature they were reading. We would visit the American Wing, select our favorite works of art, and set about describing them. But was I really making the most of this learning experience? My answer came on one of the bus trips, when I found myself responding through poetry to the churches, buildings, and bridges on our trip up the New Jersey Turnpike to the Lincoln Tunnel. What might I do to inspire students to respond (intellectually and emotionally) to what they saw in the American Wing? I began to make a list of paintings, stained glass, and sculpture in the American Wing, and, running out of time, simply listed the names of American artists, since many were represented by several works.

On our next trip, I decided to distribute the list during the bus ride. I asked students to

- select a work by each artist listed
- describe the work as specifically as they could in a sentence or two

Within the first few minutes of our arrival at the museum, my students were as excited as young children on their first scavenger hunt. They collaborated to locate the works, while I strolled around the American Wing answering questions and enjoying my own participation in the game. As we boarded the bus for the short ride to the Frick, the students were even more excited.

"What are we going to do at the Frick?" they asked.

"Any suggestions?"

"Come up with something a bit more creative," they answered.

The Frick Museum had been a private home for many years, and the dining room table still displayed a magnificent centerpiece of fresh flowers, just as it must have when the building was a family residence. I suggested the following task:

> Pretend that this is your home and you have just been told that you will have to part with all the possessions except three works of art. Select the three you want to keep and tell why you want to keep them. Don't worry about the size or the monetary value of your selections.

Students began knocking into each other in their eagerness to get off the bus and into the Frick ahead of their peers. (Once I began the same writing assignment, I realized what a difficult task I had proposed. My final choices were two paintings and a larger-than-life sculpture of Venus.) And we had to pull some students almost literally from the museum to get them home on schedule.

During the next week, I joined students as they worked on these two assignments. The students realized that their writing was as important as the works of art they had viewed at the Metropolitan and the Frick. It was a way of reflecting on their own experiences. Before, they had taken notes on the slides we viewed or the pictures they saw at the museum by rote, but now they were relating images to their own experience and communicating their ideas clearly on paper. They were eager to share their writing with their peers and eventually with me. Students wanted to become "coauthors" with the artist. Rather than just react to a painting, they wanted to participate with the artist by exploring the impact a work evokes. The artist uses the visual medium, and students wanted to respond in one of their own—words. They had engaged in a personal dialogue with a visual work, and now they were creating a text to validate that dialogue (Adams 1985; Scholes 1989). Their visual experience had moved into their own private worlds. They were more concerned about the quality of their writing because they believed their opinions were important.

Dawn published the following poem in the school literary magazine, *The Crow's Nest*:

The Portrait

Her long auburn hair is hidden
by roses and lace.
Her pale brow wrinkles slightly
In a questioning manner.
Her green eyes dance in the light,
From beneath long dark lashes.
Her Roman nose turns up
To scoff at life.
Her full red mouth frozen
In a twittering snicker.
Her ivory shoulders thrown back
In arrogant pride.
Her blue brocade frock barely visible
Under the wooden frame.
The rest is hidden . . .
"Lady Ashley."

In the same issue of *The Crow's Nest*, Elizabeth Kahn described her choice at the Frick Museum, Degas' *Woman in a Tub*. "Motherhood still lingers in the golden light of her hair. A shadow of pain crosses her face. She is still a woman, another child may come, [and] a golden glow promises everything."

This annual trip, and variations on the assignments, became part of the required curriculum for American literature, and over the next eight years or so, all the juniors participated. (If we had lived more than an hour from New York City, we would have found another museum or art gallery closer to home and used its collection to encourage writing in response to visual media.) Through individual conferences and annual course evaluations, I learned that students never tired of the adventure or of the creative excitement of writing in response to visual images. I made sure that the students were involved in devising our writing activities, which tended to be student-centered. They came to see me as a student, too, because I participated in and learned from their writing activities.

Since those early writing assignments involving the visual arts, I have tried many other projects that help students of all ages with writing. I don't believe in using such assignments as filler for days when I have nothing better to do or before or after a vacation. (I've watched colleagues show films on Fridays, and fill class time with visual material that has nothing to do with the learning involved in the course or in students' lives.) My point is quite clear:

the visual arts become a means of taking all of us beyond one art form, the written word, and of adding a wealth of texture through words.

Students end up communicating much more than they could discover otherwise. The integration of the visual and the verbal enables the writer and the reader to communicate more clearly on the same channel, or maybe I should say, the same operating system. As I study movements, such as the Pre-Raphaelite Brotherhood, I am reminded of how the visual and the written work hand in hand, from paint brush to pen and vice versa.

A Connection with Art and Writing

I remember one exchange I never would have had if it hadn't been for art. Katie was a sullen girl in my honors-level American literature class. I knew she had to be intelligent in order to meet the entry requirements, but she had yet to demonstrate much in her succinct oral responses and terse pieces of prose. In the third week of school, I introduced daily journal writing. Sometimes I gave a prompt as a thought-provoking lead for a class discussion on a new literary period, a literary device, or a connection among several works we had been reading. Most of the time we would just spend five to ten minutes writing, and sometimes longer, if necessary. After a few weeks, this bright group of students learned to use these journal times for freewrites, allowing them to escape the pressures of the difficult academic schedules they were carrying. I indicated to the class, since I wrote with them, that I was willing at anytime to participate in a dialogue journal with anyone.

One day Katie walked into class as the bell rang, dropped her books in a pile on top of her desk facing mine, and just stared at me. I wrote in my journal, "Want to talk about it?" and shoved it toward her. She looked at my writing, smirked, and responded, "I don't want to talk about it right now, but this is kind of neat." Before I read this message, Katie had begun sketching in her journal and chuckling to herself. Finally, she returned my journal and passed hers over for me to see. I can't reproduce her drawings exactly, but Figure 3–1 gives some idea of Katie's message.

My reaction to her sketches started both of us laughing and ended

Figure 3–1
Katie's drawing #1

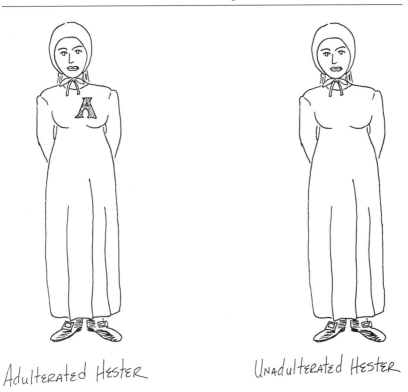

Adulterated Hester   Unadulterated Hester

any chance of further journal writing for that day. I realized that when Katie could not put her feelings into words, she could communicate through her art. Throughout the year, she let me know when it was time to talk with her pictures rather than her words. As she moved from that form of dialogue to written communication, her oral communicative skills developed, too. A girl who had been a loner, considered an "artsy" silent type, soon became a respected, actively verbal member of the class community. Other students called upon her artistic talents, and the two of us covered a lot of ground in our dialogue journal during the year. Katie feared that her parents were going to move again; the house she had loved, within walking distance of the school, was replaced with a condo on the ocean, miles from school and her few friends. She feared what would happen after her senior year, even questioning whether her parents would pay for her to go to college. I took Katie to our school psychologist and stayed with her as long as she needed me there. Later, in class, she sketched during our class discussion, a funny grin across her face. I couldn't wait to finish talking about *A Farewell to Arms*, never one of my favorites. As the bell rang, Katie put something similar to the sketch in Figure 3–2 on my desk and called from the doorway, "See ya tomorrow, Mrs. Farrell [Childers]."

Katie has since moved on to a career as an artist after getting a scholarship to Rutgers. We haven't seen each other in years, but other students have told me she's doing fine. Would Katie have broken through those communication barriers without her art? I don't know, but I do know that she was able to become an active communicator through her art, her words, and her voice by the end of the year. The sense of humor apparent in her art added another element to her ability to get her message across to a real audience, me.

Figure 3–2
Katie's drawing #2

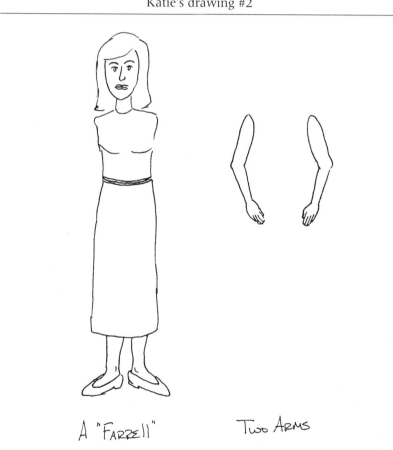

A "Farrell"   Two Arms

Still Life and Poetry

A few years ago my poetry class was invited to visit art teacher Catherine Neuhardt-Minor's art studio. Here she had created a still life to give art students a sense of perspective in their drawing. The two sides of the still life had latticework in front of them. Through either end (or through sections of the lattice), one could observe a platform holding the following objects, all draped with cobwebs:

- a snowshoe rocker with a shawl draped over it
- a stuffed snake
- a gold pump
- artist's brushes in a pottery pitcher
- a stuffed raccoon on a tree stump

Students were given no directions for their writing other than to observe from whatever place they wished to stand or sit and to begin writing whatever came to mind. What occurred went far beyond classroom interaction and discussion. Somehow the still life triggered imaginative, creative poetry far beyond any they had previously written. Here are some excerpts:

> The vines seep through the hole in the attic.
> The dust and cobwebs
> make the life in here die.
> But, this place will always be alive
> to me.

> Once upon a time.
> Fairies lose their innocence, . . .
> Grimm drinks bourbon by the pint . . .
> Imagination isn't useful, because everything is real.
> Our babies are old.

I question whether these students would have considered such thoughts or written them down without this three-dimensional visual experience. I tried the same activity the following year, and Catherine produced an even more challenging still life. It had a variety of objects, including

- an American flag
- some gardening tools
- empty picture frames hanging from a tool rack

Recently, a colleague who is an artist and a poet explained how she felt compelled to create a painting based on a poem that another friend had written. When she finished, she was inspired to write her own poem based on her painting. Things didn't end there, however, because her new poem triggered the creation of still another painting. Perhaps, for her, the cycle will never end. When one is multitalented, visual and verbal art continue to inspire each other. For most of us, however, it is the visual world around us, the visual art of others, and the pictures we create in our mind that inspire our written responses. Although we may be surrounded by visual images, so often we don't stop to consider or look at our responses.

The Environment

It is important to create a classroom environment within which the following can happen:

- Students are offered visual stimulation.
- Students have a place to talk and write about that visual experience.
- Students have an opportunity to share the experience in public.

Certainly I would encourage students to tune in to their other senses for inspiration. But everyone *sees* in the transcendental sense. When someone says, "I see," they mean I understand or I comprehend. In talking about revision, Donald Murray refers to it as "re-vision," meaning to understand or comprehend in a new way. Murray himself understands the uses of the visual in written communication (see Figure 3–3).

Every day we should remember to bring in the visual, not only to stimulate our students' writing but also to help them "re-vision" their world and revise it. If they are having trouble using details, we can say, "Look around this room, then close your eyes and tell me what you saw." We write those details on the board or have students type them into a computer. "Now, look again and see all the details you have missed. Then look at your piece of writing and give your reader the same kind of details." For teachers in subjects across the disciplines the visual arts can stimulate new ways of seeing, writing, and thinking. The visual and cultural contexts students experience on trips to museums create a rich personal environment for verbal explorations.

Figure 3–3
Donald Murray's sketch

Writing

The poet must learn
the terrible patience of the heron

the slow, dainty steps toward the yet unseen
and, yes, the sudden cruel strike

but most of all the calm
waiting

the certainty
of prey.

Donald M. Murray

Response

JOAN A. MULLIN

Pam Childers' comment, "although we may be surrounded by visual images, so often we don't stop to look" points to the main reason I think her suggestions prove valuable: The activities make students look and have several benefits for the instructor.

- *It's a motivator:* Pam's suggestions to get students out of the familiar classroom usually stimulates interest and motivation. Too often students don't *see* anymore in a classroom that has grown generic and predictable (as a result, they don't *hear* anymore or *do* anymore either).

- *It connects learning to the world:* Students don't often connect what they study to their lives outside school walls. The *outside* world moves too fast for students to concentrate on a single image or idea. Moving to a place that challenges the eye, slows the response, and makes them assess their reaction not only produces good thinking and good writing, it is a lesson that transfers to other issues in and out of a class. Pam's methods here force connections by sharpening observation.

- *Materials are accessible:* What materials may be needed (for the still life activity) are readily available. The lattice itself, for example, can be replaced by a piece of grillwork, premade fencing, or a trellis, and the effect can also be achieved by restricting the view with cardboard boxes, curtains, scarves, shower curtains, or lace curtains.

- *Activities are adaptable to different places and different levels of students:* The second writing activity Pam mentions—choosing and writing about pieces of art you would save—can be conducted in any kind of setting that arrests the eye: a museum, a historical society, a historical district, a landmark home. The writing task can even be adapted to a botanical garden or a display of insects, butterflies, or birds. Directions can be as complex or simple as you want to make them.

- *Activities are adaptable to a variety of purposes:* As Pam points out, students responded enthusiastically (they were motivated to write), they reworked their pieces (revision), and they revised together (collaboration, peer editing).

Thematic Variations

Parts of a Paper

I once worked with studio art students who gave me a rich, concrete, visual vocabulary. Art students speak about what "color," "tone," "line," or "shadow" mean in relation to the particular medium in which they work. They already understand that every work draws the eye to a focal point and that from every focal point the eye ranges across an artwork, usually in a fairly predictable order based on the arrangement of figures, light, shapes, or movements. The visual elements students already used in their artistic productions—focus, organization, tone, style, and color—seemed to correspond easily to similar abstract elements of writing a paper. Explaining style, audience, or even organization was less difficult once I began drawing the relationship between the concrete definitions familiar to artists and those same terms as they applied to written texts. As usual, it was a student who showed me the value of this visual vocabulary.

A few years ago I was particularly struck by one art student's layering of detail in a paper, detail that went nowhere and had no main purpose showing me why I should read all of it. In a casual conversation with her studio art instructor, I discovered that she had a similar problem in her visual productions: her canvases gave details similar weight and provided no focal points, nowhere for the eye to rest. While this chaos could have been another artist's intention, it was not this student's, and she often complained that no one understood her work.

Keeping the art instructor's diagnosis in mind, I began to use the student's sketch book to talk about focal point, organization, and perspective in a verbal work. She began to *see* my point, and her papers gained new solidity and linearity as a result. (I often wish I had followed up by asking whether this instruction proved useful in solving her visual chaos, but I didn't.)

What I have since realized is that students in our culture have already been introduced to the basics of art through animation, commercials, ads, and slick media productions. They know the value of a commercial that grabs attention with innovative use of color, visual detail, and a focal point that repeats in each frame. After a trip to the museum, where students have closely observed artwork, they will develop a culturally rich visual vocabulary for talking about what they see. Teachers can capitalize on their prior knowledge by using that vocabulary to describe the "color," "tone," "focal point," or "spatial organization" of their ideas. They easily get the picture.

Parts of a Paper (Another Version)

Students develop their own visual vocabulary. They can do this, of course, before visiting a museum by looking at advertisements, music videos, book or CD covers, or commercials. As Pam's chapter shows, it is advantageous to guide students through such an experience with questions, and similarly, a preexercise can arm them with a visual vocabulary. However, the activity is flexible enough to suit many time frames and objectives, and can wait until after the visit. Although every class list will most likely be quite similar, we know about the positive learning effects that result when students discover their own vocabularies, their own knowledge. Therefore, whether before or after the trip to the museum, students can take the visual vocabulary they have developed and apply it by naming corresponding parts of their paper.

I suggest that students work together on this. Each visual medium has similar techniques for persuading, demonstrating, or analyzing, so students do not have to have chosen similar pieces for their descriptive text. Each group can focus on an area of their choice. What you will get may resemble what usually turns up: beginning, middle, and end (where the eye travels); transitions (jump edits, color, space); use of key words or phrases (repetitious form, or the catch phrase for emphasis); the main point (focal point); point of view (camera angle, perspective). You don't have to be an art expert; because of TV (especially music videos), movies, commercials, and endless audio and visual reviews of these media, the words students need are already part of their familiar lexicon. The result? Those who are more visual will be able to *see* a map for a written paper; those who are more verbal will understand why abstract ideas need to be supported with concrete details.

One More Step

The writing students produce can further their understanding of both written and visual texts, with an end to improving their production and analysis of both. Student works can be bound together into a classroom text (made easier by desktop publishing, though that is not a necessary tool). Few people understand the art of the book, even though it affects all of us who read. By producing a book of their own work, we teach them that the form and format in which information is contained controls the knowledge it holds. Students will have to make layout decisions: Poetry first, then short descriptions? Pictures or no pictures? What about the contents of the book: Does everyone get published? In what order? Alphabetical order of last names? Best to worst? And who judges? Discussions about such decisions inevitably lead to copyright issues and a consideration of plagiarism.

Teachable moments continue throughout this publishing experience. While students are engaged in the production of their own book, they can be looking at their textbooks and other books, ostensibly to get ideas. But the classroom conversations can revolve around issues of text and graphic production. The teacher can bring in some old textbooks and have students compare the number of pictures in newer books to that in similar but older texts: What does the obvious increase mean: Better production? Easier technology? Dependence on the quick learning opportunity offered by a visual? Students should also look at fonts and page layout, two important visual effects that most of us often fail to notice even though they play a vital role in our attitude toward the information thus contained.

In some classes, students will want to include their own drawings; in others that will create problems: Color? Size? Ratio of text to art? Other questions arise: What are the costs of color? How does that influence whether a publisher includes visual elements in a book or not? Who determines what is published? On what grounds? Merit only? In one composition class we got so involved in this conversation, I was afraid the quarter would pass us by without much student writing to show for it. Then they turned in their journals. As I had asked, each night they had responded to a prompt derived from the kinds of questions that were generated in class discussions. It became apparent that students had enjoyed writing their personal responses and that each student had the makings of a complete description of what a book could and couldn't be.

Their final project, therefore, was to make a book out of all their work that was pertinent to our central question: Visually and verbally, what makes a good book? Their own "books" were to exemplify their visual and verbal ideas with only one constraint: each had to have an opening "introduction," an argument for the work contained therein, that explained what I would see and why I would see it. Students included journal entries, essays, creative papers, drawings, copies of pages from books (new and old), various text styles and layout styles. The formats ranged from the handsewn book to the three-ring binder. Nonetheless, one discovery seemed consistent: students pointed out that the book's format should depend upon the content. I regret not having any examples, because they demonstrate a deeper understanding of writing and the visual than the work of other classes I have previously taught, but these college students picked up their final projects because they wanted to keep them!

Dia-graphing

Pam's use of the drawing-writing dialogue journal gave me another idea. Although I have always encouraged students to draw in their journals or to ignore the straight lines if they choose to, I'm usually the only one doing so as I comment on their work. I think that next time I'll devote at least one class to a collaborative project in which students cannot talk. Using the dialogue journal as their resource, students will have to create a layout for an infomercial. If this works the way I think it will, the ensuing discussion should provide experiential instruction on collaboration, brainstorming, and using the journal as a resource, and will demonstrate the kinds of boundaries one can break when combining the visual and verbal in a journal.

Now You See Me . . .

Finally, Pam's writing exercise employing the still life with latticework seems a treasure trove of lessons in both visual and verbal perspective and interpretation: Each student's analysis of the still life depends on his or her position in the room. It also provides a jumping-off point for discussing multicultural writers (such as Sandra Cisneros, Toni Morrison, Nellie Wong, Amado Muro, Dave Martin Nez). As the texts of these writers show, each person's interpretation of life depends on the experiences they undergo and how those experiences are layered upon, placed next to, or separated by other experiences. This exercise shows that some people are very good at *bending* or extending their view, anticipating where a vine ends in the lattice, what the other side of the raccoon looks like, or how the snowshoe hidden under the cloth is shaped. What students quickly discover though, is that their ability to see a whole picture is limited to where they sit in the classroom (that is, in society).

Students can use their still life papers to create a larger vision in the classroom: each work can be copied and then *mapped* on a wall according to the student's physical relationship to the lattice. Ideally, the map would be formed around a pier or a column so those reading it could verbally experience the visual point of view experienced by the students. This physical exemplification of the importance of point of view and experience could not only stimulate an introductory discussion on multicultural literature, but it could eventually be transformed into a concrete touchstone for some of the writing practices we already ask of our students.

A common assignment is to write a paper from two different perspectives or to analyze a play from the point of view of a minor character or characters (Tom Stoppard's *Rosencrantz and Guildenstern Are Dead* is an excellent example). Yet once these creative exercises are over, students often don't carry over what they have learned about point of view to other work. Or, as we have discovered in our writing centers, students write from another perspective just to please the teacher. Too often we hear students saying, "Well, I have to say that because it's what my teacher wants to hear." They achieve no thoughtful integration of new information, nor do they attempt to support a personal perspective.

The resulting papers are poorly constructed, lack coherence, are short on evidence, and often contain surface errors that point to a lack of engagement in the assignment. But what if a precondition to writing was the knowledge that by dint of each writer's perspective—their place in front of the lattice—their point of view would be different from another's? For students, this exercise underscores the point of a multicultural unit or course—that different experiences produce different points of view—while encouraging students to explore the conditions that shape their own perspectives.

Now You See Me, Now You Don't

I would suggest that, before beginning a multicultural unit, students experience an exercise like Pam's, in which they have to work their way through visual layers that depend upon a particular point of view, in which they have to wrestle with color, balance, space, shape, figure, and background. Then they can write a paper proposing a particular perspective: it can be a creative or a descriptive essay, but in some way (for example, visually, emotionally) it must recreate what it is they see. Next, assign a paper written from the point of view of someone else. These two could be pasted or stacked over the visual pieces to form a verbal latticework. In creating this *verbal* still life, students would have to discuss the papers, their point of view in terms of what they see, what they don't see, what is missing and why, what they need to look at more closely. The next step, of course, is for them to present their own perspective on a work of literature. The visual latticework could stop at this point—or continue.

Postscript

All these exercises support "re-vision": they supply models or visual cues that serve as guidelines for analysis. Mostly though, these activities help students extend a visual experience into a learning experience. New research in neuroscience suggests that the visual supports the verbal wiring of the brain, which would mean that visual experiences reinforce verbal/cognitive skills. These exercises, in which the visual and the spatial complement instruction, move students enthusiastically to verbal communication and seem to help them retain a verbal understanding and facility within various areas of our discipline. The potential application to other disciplines lies in manipulating the visual experience (see Chapter 6), the subject of the dialogue journals, or the objects behind the latticework. Just as the museum holds potential for our students, these activities hold potential for our pedagogy.

Alternative Pedagogy
Visualizing Theories of Composition

JOAN A. MULLIN

Working with Dick Putney in architecture classes like the one
he describes in Chapter 6 fed my long-time interest in architecture, but they also offered a ground for my growing interest in the connections between the visual and verbal. As the writing
expert in the class, I asked Dick what it was that his students had difficulty understanding in these classes. He immediately said that they
lacked the ability to observe detail. Students in his classes would learn
basic Gothic architectural concepts like buttress, clerestory, and so on,
or could easily learn them because they had probably heard these
terms before, but they did not become adept at identifying the subtle
differences that distinguished particular periods of time, cultures, or
regions. The traditional art historian's methods, lecture and slideshow,
did not accomplish as much as he hoped. What we had to do was create a bridge from the concrete, physical, visual, graphic world to an abstract, intangible, textual, imaginative one. An initial, successful use of
architectural language to discuss writing brought me closer to finding a
solution to this problem and to answering a question that kept emerging for me: despite our emphasis on process writing, why do students
increasingly seem to write less interesting, in-depth papers?

Somewhere during the Gothic architecture class I started using
the language of architecture to talk about how to write a paper.
Terms referring to cathedral structure—the nave, rotating chapels,
center aisle, clerestory—became metaphors for the writing process:
focus, main argument, radiating arguments. For example, buttressing

arguments, like their architectural counterparts, seem to support the weight of the paper (building) invisibly; there is a seamless series of claims and assumptions that form the structure underneath the main point (the vault of the ceiling) upon which one builds. Nonetheless, as buttresses emerge on the outside of a building, so too do concrete arguments that one can see within the paper. For students so immersed in learning architectural terminology, such language proved a convenient and beneficial way to talk about the dual purposes of the course: to teach writing and to teach Gothic architecture. What I began to learn in this class, however, led me to develop a metaphor that has proved useful in many of my classes. The process draws together the physical, visual world of the students and the abstract, textual world of the classroom, so they *see* the writing process.

A New Si(gh)t(e)

After I had completed several class collaborations with Dick, an event occurred that uprooted the entire art department and offered an opportunity to use architectural language to teach students about writing in classes other than art history. The university art department had always been housed in the Toledo Museum of Art. Considered one of the ten best in the country, the museum looks, well, like a museum: its nineteenth-century-schooled architect created a Greek temple to art in the midst of a graceful residential area (Figure 4–1).

Today, however, while the columned facade of the museum faces graceful restored mansions, the back looks over the roaring traffic of Interstate I-75 and beyond that, a mostly African American neighborhood struggling to keep itself above poverty. Likewise, the museum was struggling through a capital campaign to renovate galleries and renew its art education program in the community, and planned to reclaim the offices and classrooms formerly dedicated to the art department. As part of the renovation, a new art department building would be constructed next to the museum. After a competitive review of submissions by architects, the contract was given to Frank Gehry, one of the most controversial internationally known postmodern (though he dislikes the term) creators of space today. Once the controversy about the daring design died down in Toledo, the resulting CVA (Center for Visual Arts) became the centerpiece for Dick's new class on postmodern architecture (Figures 4–2 and 4–3).

Students were ambivalent about the new building for many reasons. They were leaving the very familiar, very solid museum in which they had long been housed. Many saw the new CVA as a disruptive space, difficult to move into and even more difficult to get

Figure 4–1
Toledo Museum of Art

Figure 4–2
Center for Visual Arts (front)

Figure 4–3
Center for Visual Arts (back)

used to. They were simultaneously drawn to and repelled by it. As students voiced their response to the building during class and in their journals, their words took on a predictable ring. More and more I found that I could substitute "writing" for "CVA": "I don't like the CVA [writing] because it's not a building [paper] one can easily describe [write about]." Dick was frustrated by the students' inability to lay aside their assumptions and write about the building with insight. As the tension in class increased, I was frustrated because when we did ask students to write, they were turning in fairly *safe* papers:

- the ones that are five paragraphs in nature
- the sort that tell us what students think we want
- the ones that leave out as much of their personal views as possible
- the kind that skim the surface
- the ones always preceded in class by someone asking, "And how long does this have to be?"

As Dick and I talked about the class, the museum, and the CVA, I began to see the two structures as more than a metaphor for writing; they served as visual, physical examples of the differences between how students may have been taught to write and how they now needed to learn to write.

Traditional Architecture, Traditional Writing

The days I took over the class to talk about writing, I explored this metaphor with students. While we had the physical buildings to walk through as well as slides, I have since found that either one will do. The following is a blueprint of what we discussed and its correspondences to writing. The objective behind this teaching strategy was to have students visually and physically *walk through* two different, built spaces and compare those experiences to writing within different contexts. High school students can easily relate to this exercise, and its feasibility is evident from the way in which educators are speaking about successfully using architecture as metaphor and content in elementary classrooms. For these teachers, as for me, architecture is a natural connection because it has "two distinct design traditions: building as concept and building as construction. On the one hand the building is seen as the realization of a set of ideas about the philosophy of beauty, symbology and the nature of space, human interaction and place. On the other, the building is an assembly of materials that are jointed, finished and positioned to protect and promote human activity" (Cleaver, Scheurer, and Shorey 1993, 354).

This definition corresponds easily to "two distinct design traditions" in writing: that associated with content and that associated with conventions. Neither can exist without the other, although educational tradition in English has caused many students (and teachers) to think about the two as mutually exclusive (giving one grade for content and one for grammar; teaching grammar in isolation from the act of writing and the contexts in which one writes; assuming that once students have learned grammar they can write; assuming that if students cannot write, we should teach more conventions and grammar). That tradition, unfortunately, is often maintained at the expense of students. They learn that they cannot write unless they know the comma rule. Or *never*, under any circumstances, to start a sentence with "and" or "or." And, of course, they learn that length determines how much one says, rather than content determining how much room one needs to say it. Thus, to get back to the architecture class, when they find themselves challenged by new ideas, they revert to old forms rather than using the new ideas to determine how they might write in the new context. If this last sentence is abstract and confusing, so it was to the students, and thus I started one class by showing slides of the museum. Later, students actually walked through the two spaces, comparing them on their own. The following is a collapsed version of the correspondences we found between the museum (see Figure 4–4) and the CVA and between traditional and contemporary views about writing.

Figure 4–4
Toledo Museum of Art footprint

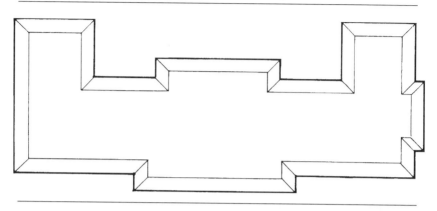

Museum (Original design)	Writing (Traditional approach)
Large, formal, ornate entrance facing major street and newly restored residential area of turn-of-the-century mansions. The entrance is framed, decorated, and obvious.	Begin your essay with a catchy introduction that will interest the reader. Do not insult the reader, but make sure that your thesis is the last sentence of the introduction.
After walking up the long staircase and through the doors, one stands in the entryway and then walks through to the central lobby. Containing one graceful sculpture in the middle, the open space soars overhead and the floor indicates choices: left or right to the galleries, or straight ahead to whatever special exhibit is currently showing. Though the staircases (subtly placed behind columns) indicate	The first paragraph should indicate how your essay will proceed and give the reader a clear indication of what you will present. Often there are three clear supporting points arranged in corresponding paragraphs. Let your reader know what these will be and in what order they will be presented. If necessary, dismiss any items that may prevent your reader from understanding your main

a downstairs, no one would mistake the implication that these lead to services: restrooms, stores, dining, and educator's resources.

points: that is, narrow your topic sufficiently so that the reader does not bring in biased or extraneous views.

There are no windows
to the outside
once a visitor enters the
museum. No matter which
direction one chooses (right,
left, or center), one
will always have
to return to the lobby
to move to another area.

Whatever point you choose
to start with,
continually relate it to
your main point. Make
sure you have clear transitions
between each paragraph. Your
focus should be tight and
not cause a reader to stray
from the main point.

At the end of the museum
visit, or at any
time visitors return to the lobby,
they can use the services
downstairs. When they
wish to leave, however, they
will do so through the
main lobby upstairs.

Make sure not only that
you support your
main points, but that
you anticipate objections
others may raise or
give examples of support
(there are many
correspondences to *services*).
Always, however, return
to your main point.

Visitors exit the same way
they came.

Be sure to restate your main
point in the conclusion.

The purpose of a museum
is to display
already created
pieces of art that have
been deemed *masterpieces*.

The purpose of a paper
is to display an already
formulated argument or point of
view (such as a description).
When it is submitted, it should
be a finished, perfect piece.

Just as we can usually pick out the post office or the courthouse in any small town, so too, the museum (and the traditional paper) has specific parts that one expects to see and use in particular ways. This arrangement presupposes a familiarity with convention and the culture that produced it (I would not, for example, assume to know the first thing about entering or finding my way through a temple in Bali). Likewise, teachers presuppose that students are familiar enough with school culture to put information where it is expected in the way they expect it. As a result, the emphasis in a paper is on display, on ideas being in the right order in the right place. The museum is not intended to explore the ways art might be conceived, or even to consider unacceptable productions that aspire to be called art (museums don't purchase pieces not already recognized as valuable in the art world). Likewise, though we talk about the importance of students' ideas and emphasize process in our classrooms, the *form* in which we demand our students' texts *really* announces to them: *We want a reproduction of already accepted ideas—ours—in acceptable formats.*

(Post)modern Architecture, (Post)modern Writing Process

The process movement of the seventies was to have changed all that, but teachers' own upbringing often placed (and still places) a wedge between what they speak about in class and the message they give students through feedback on papers: unintentional though it may be, our evaluation and assessment practices encourage traditional approaches. Then we wonder why students don't take risks, why they write *safe*—and boring—papers, or why they don't even know grammar (though we may like their ideas). This gets right back to the problem in the architecture class: faced with a challenging subject, students couldn't find a form or format for exploring their ideas. And if they tried to circumscribe the tension between what they thought and what they wrote by turning in a traditional paper, one of two things happened: their form was weak (the paper had lots of syntactical or grammar errors) or their format suffered (the paper was disorganized, inconclusive, or lacked support). This is where constructing a comparison with the CVA for students proved useful. (See Figure 4–5.)

CVA (Postmodern)

Writing (Process)

The logical entryway for this building would be the same as the museum: facing the major road through town and the residential neighborhood. However, the only thing that greets the eye on that *side* of the building is a number of planes and curves flowing and jutting in and out of each

Nowadays, papers can't always start the way they used to. While it may be visually obvious that what one is holding is a text, sometimes a lot of background must precede any major *point*. This may be due to the emphasis on narrative or point of view. But, as with

Figure 4–5
CVA footprint

other. As one walks around, one sees in the building a wing that juts like the prow of a ship (a reference to Toledo as a shipping center on Lake Erie), the suggestion of a cathedral (a nod to the one down the street and the others on the horizon). One has to move around the entire building to get to the entrance in what could easily be called the back. While there is an entrance, as one would expect in a building, it's not exactly in the place one might expect. And one can enter the center of the building through a glass enclosed courtyard next to the common entryway.

The front of the building is composed of rectangular copper lead sheeting that mimics, in its blockiness,

this chapter and this book, we increasingly find that we can't assume our audience comes from the same (gracious, nineteenth century?) background; we need to make connections between our ideas, show where they come from, and bring our audience to these reference points before we get to the main point(s). As with the CVA, there may be more than one point of entry: one, obvious, the other, subtler, equal in importance.

The introduction of a process paper, though it may not contain the main point, is nonetheless a beginning.

the slabs of marble that
make up the museum next to it.
Planes angle off in juxtaposition
with the museum's roof line. And
where the front is a solid mass
broken with windows, the back—
the entrance—is all glass.

Embedded in it are expectations
that this text, like others, will
lead the reader to an expected
point of entry. There will be
sentences, they will be *correct*,
and the grammar and structure
will be used to accomplish
an obvious end. Previously
unthinkable, it is now not
unusual to read "in this
paper, I will explore" or
"I would like to look at . . ."

The visitor has choices at
the entrance, though usually, the
complexity of the courtyard
entry in relation to the
building is passed up for
the clearly familiar entryway
with large doors.

One can be well into the paper
before a main point emerges,
but the main point will,
nonetheless, clearly stand out.

There are choices after
passing though the entryway:
left or right. A glance
left immediately shows a
gallery for student art—and a
wall with a large door in it.
This door signifies the end
of the CVA on that side,
but walking through the
door will bring a person into a
long, curving corridor that
leads into the museum.

It is not unusual for process
papers to use research,
the already accepted ideas
of others, as part of the
paper. These citations might
lead to further ones and
even to a recommended
bibliography. Some space
might be devoted to going
over the pertinent research
that led to the present
text. But mostly, in a process
paper, the reader, like the
writer, wants to see what the
writer thinks.

If one turns to the left, there
stretches a long corridor with
the glass of the courtyard
on one side, a wall on
the other, doors to stairs,
rest rooms, department
offices, and then, the

The process text unfolds,
usually exposing the writer's
way of thinking, how she
approached the subject, why he
chose this area, and how the
reader might participate in
constructing the meaning of

elevators and museum library
way at the end; however, one
also sees, through the glass
and courtyard, that the
corridor turns right and forms
another corridor. What's down
there? There is a playfulness
of beckoning corridors, shifts
in perspective, angled walls;
a visitor wants to explore
and is invited to do so.

Despite the soaring ceiling,
the glass, and the playful
perspectives offered by the
architectural design, the visitor
is in a familiar corridor that
leads to familiar, useful
spaces: the department
offices, student gallery,
stairwells, elevators, library.
All the pieces are there,
but juxtaposed differently,
causing one to reconsider
their placement and,
therefore, their functions in
the production of art.

Wherever one wants
to go in the CVA, there
are several ways to
do so—or so it appears.
One continually feels the need
to explore this building and
is for the most part invited to

the text: you are invited to play
with the ideas, write in the
margins, argue with the text,
suspend your disbelief, reflect
on the words alone and on your
responses to those words.
You are invited to interact
with the text.

There are choices for
writers that may displace
their readers' expectations.
The sentences in a paper
may be organized syntactic
units, and they may offer
evidence or give examples.
Yet writers are playing with
punctuation, risking more
by presenting personal
points of view and
multiple perspectives.
While texts today may
lay out major arguments
beforehand, they
don't always do so. Readers
will be led through a text by
familiar signs, marks, transitions,
summaries, and restatements;
however, the formatting of
a text may also make
use of desktop publishing
possibilities: ideas may
be physically juxtaposed.

A process paper may
seem exploratory, but
reader and writer
should both have a clear
sense of its purpose. Eventually,
all discussions in the paper
are pertinent to the entire

do so (the drawing and painting studios had to put up signs asking visitors to respect the classes in session, because they kept wandering in). There are wonderful nooks and crannies offering framed window views of the surrounding grassy area and downtown skyline to the east, of the museum's architecture to the west, of the expressway and neighborhood beyond to the south, and of the major street and residences beyond to the north, and even a surprise tiny balcony. Nonetheless, in order to exit, there are only some obvious choices, and one takes precedence: the main entryway.

environment being created for the reader. The writer may offer possible areas for further exploration, acknowledge that more research is needed, or state that she is making a generalization for the purposes of this discussion and knows it, but there is still a reason behind writing papers and it is often to offer one perspective on a subject—that is, not necessarily a definitive answer, but one particular perspective held by the writer for the reasons just constructed. While the reader may have a personal perspective or discover new ideas in the text, the writer is offering this view at this time.

In the CVA, art is created, risks taken, ideas explored, lines redrawn, perspectives moved.

Conclusions may suggest, question, offer further areas of investigation. Answers are not necessarily given, and, if given, not definitive. This set of ideas contributes to a pool of ever-changing knowledge.

Laying the Groundwork for Change

One could say that this activity lends itself only to art history or art classes. On my own, I would not have shown pictures of these buildings to students and said, "Okay, now, how are these buildings like writing?" That this visualization worked at all testifies to the power of Dick's perspective and knowledge when joined to my experience and perception. Yet it seems that in our classes we often ask students to move from the verbalized museum they bring to our classrooms to a very different CVA verbalization. Unfortunately, we do it without clearly demonstrating that they must undergo a "paradigm shift." Students—and, too often, teachers—aren't aware that reading a textbook or hearing a discussion about a new concept does not always ensure that learning will take place. Students often have to see that their own long-ingrained and previously held ideas will cause them to continue responding in traditional ways. Physically comparing the museum (or any traditional building) to a new space provides a visual context for discussing the world of ideas students hold and the one into which we want them to move.

Mina Shaughnessy, Langer, Vygotsky, and others studying language acquisition have pointed out that the child's interpretation of language and the way it works begins long before formal schooling. Children begin with a visual vocabulary before proceeding to a textual one. If the perceptions (speaking visually and cognitively) underlying students' ideas remain stuck in a former way of thinking, learning, or doing, processing new information will not displace their previously held ideas. I ask students to picture their already constructed world as a sieve. As new knowledge comes in, some remains trapped but some slips through. Our constructed world (the sieve) will only retain information that it can accommodate; all else is forgotten.

This metaphor, however imperfect, gives me a place to begin talking about why students who have had twelve years of grammar and syntax still cannot use the conventions when they write. It gives me a place to talk about why students in the writing center who don't understand how to use commas are not shown yet another copy of the rules for commas but asked, "Why did you put a comma *there?*" This question elicits the incorrect rule the student does hold: "Well, every sentence has to have a comma" (this is a true response from a student). That's the teachable moment. Similarly, unless we bring students to an understanding of how they think about writing and about constructing texts, we will find it difficult to move them toward a more mature writing that exhibits critical thinking. Instead of visiting the museum, they will be stuck there for the duration.

Offering a Blueprint to Students

By leading students through two different structures, I was able to have them discuss their writing in terms of architectural differences. Although this strategy may not appeal to every teacher and such radically different buildings may not be available in every town, certain elements of this activity can be successfully adapted. For example,

1. As a class, draw a "footprint" (the surface area it covers) of the school or a building on campus; have students determine what they expect inside, and where they expect it to be.

2. Every town has a courthouse or a public library that looks like what it is. Ask students to draw its footprint as they remember it and discuss their expectations about the building's design and function.

3. Have students draw a footprint of their house. How does it differ from the footprint of a public building?

4. Have students write an essay about a given topic, or choose an essay they have already written. Have them draw a footprint of their paper or that of another student.

Assignments such as these give students a pictorial representation from which they can discuss a number of writing-related issues:

How is the purpose of a building (text) announced by its form?
This leads to discussions of main points in texts (the "So what?" question), introductions, supporting evidence, description, or subsections.

What expectations do public buildings (texts) signal to their visitors (readers)?
This can address reader expectations and writer obligations, formats, and the diversity of formats across disciplines.

How do people learn what to expect from buildings (texts)?
Discussions here can range from what constitutes a "good" paper to factors contributing to students' attitudes toward writing.

What happens if some feature a visitor (reader) expects to find in a building (text) is missing?
This provides a good basis for discussing confusion on the reader's part, from organization problems, lack of conventional reading signals, surface features that lead readers to spend a lot of time trying to guess what is meant, point of view, and so on.

When can a building (text) break the rules or deviate from what is expected?
Can writers make their own rules? When?

For those students who are visual or kinesthetic learners, walking around in a building becomes a concrete metaphor for walking around in a text. For those students who are verbal learners, the discussions can clarify for them the ways in which texts need to be constructed. For all learners today, most of whom are subject to media images in one form or another, these activities open the possibility for reading other visual representations. Students

- develop a personal vocabulary for examining objects spatially
- develop a classroom vocabulary for assessment (foundation, supporting walls, detail, footprint)
- learn how readers *see* and (re)construct their written texts
- realize the impact the visual has on us even without our conscious knowledge
- acquire skills and a desire for visual analysis

Using the Gehry building as a way to discuss the structure of a paper certainly worked in that class. Since that time, I have been able to adapt the idea of the footprint successfully to other classes. Whether that alone proved crucial to the papers my students wrote—thoughtful, developed, organized, and at times, as they played with structure, risky—might be too broad a claim. I do know, however, that architecture became part of the vocabulary in our classroom as students peer-edited each other's work, as I conferred with students, and, when the year was over, students reminisced about our classes together. As one student put it, "I never understood why teachers couldn't understand what I was saying—I thought it was clear! And then I saw that my supporting structure would have been blown down by the first big bad wolf that came along! I finally could see what I was doing."

Response

PAMELA B. CHILDERS

Joan has introduced some interesting new ways of teaching writing through the language of architecture. Her discussion stimulates my interest in its applications, and I like it for several reasons.

- As Joan describes it, she and Dick wanted to "create a bridge from the concrete, physical, visual, graphic world to an abstract, intangible, textual, imaginative one." Isn't this one of the very problems we so often face as writers ourselves? As teachers of writing we embrace anything that will encourage students to *picture* what they want to say or give it some reality other than our frequently abstract prompt. Through tangible metaphors our students may begin to *see* a concept and talk about it in a different way.

- Just this morning, my husband Malcolm and I were trying to decide how to write the outline for our workshop with Michael Fatali, a professional photographer. Michael sees through a large-format camera lens in ways that I can only imagine when I look at his spectacular prints. We needed to describe our roles as collaborating workshop leaders to him as clearly as possible. I took a pen and drew three lines that rose and fell, indicating our responsibilities from day one to day five. Our roles would be unique but also connected, overlapping, and interwoven in some places during the workshop. Our friend would understand this visual representation. Now I could explain what I was trying to say because I had also made it clear to myself. I was trying out what Joan suggests in this chapter. Now I want to use it with my students before they begin their next writing assignment.

- *Using another language, the language of architecture in this case, provides a metaphoric way of talking about writing.* A research paper, like a building, has a definite structure. I would even guess that writing, like building, involves certain "building codes" that an "inspector" must check during each step of the process. Maybe using this metaphor with research papers would solve many of the problems with this dreaded unit in junior English classes.

Just this past week one of my colleagues in the history department came to me with a list of deadlines for the class research paper and asked me to explain the MLA research format and research techniques on the Internet. Now that I think about it, I will describe the research process as building a structure. My assistant and I will supervise the construction site and check students' work to see that it meets the building requirements. I'm eager to see what happens, especially regarding deadlines!

Think of the possibilities with other subjects. For example, Mike Lancaster's biology students are creating classroom-size models of organelles of a cell as conceptual works of art. Each organelle will be described in a guidebook for the classroom cell. From photography to graphs in precalculus to mapped-out battles in history, we can borrow metaphors to use in teaching writing. If we are speaking of English literature, don't we read Keats' poem, "Ode to a Nightingale," and compare the bird's song to a poem and the bird to the poet? How is a poem like the song of the nightingale? We are drawing on sound, not just sight. Having students use language from another discipline to create a workable metaphor for their writing might prove quite challenging because it requires careful observation and concentration and forces them to focus on details as they have never done before.

Of course, these metaphors do not have to derive from specific disciplines. Students could also draw a model to help them work their way through the writing process. With current technology, they could even take a virtual trip through their model. Today one of my peer tutors wrote in his journal that he was a kite, and the school gave him more string each year till the end of his senior year when the school would let go. He would have to succeed or fail on his own; what the school was trying to teach him was how to fly.

■ *Since many of us team teach courses with teachers in other disciplines, I think it is important to draw on the content of those subjects in teaching writing.* Joan and Dick combined resources to develop a new way of approaching a subject and of teaching writing. "The process draws together the physical and visual world of the students with the abstract textual world of the classroom, making them *see* the writing process," Joan says.

Recently one of my colleagues said she was surprised that her students could find little research material on Faulkner's *The Unvanquished*. She wanted them to become familiar with researching on the Internet, but she also wanted them to be able to identify and organize key ideas in what they had found and present them in a written form that demonstrated their knowledge of the novel. She came up with the idea of having the students create home pages for the novel on Microsoft FrontPage or AOL Press (Internet software). Each student would create his own home page and save it on a disk. Then the class would look at all the home pages on a large projector connected to the computer. This would enable the teacher and the class to learn about the material available together, and what is authentic, important, and relevant from the plethora of material available on the Internet. She could talk about organization, presentation, citations, and many other aspects of writing literary criticism and research papers. The words and the visuals used on the home pages would have to interact to communicate clear messages. The more I think about this assignment, the more I see a home page or web page as a new metaphor for a piece of writing. The links to other sites would be the specific details (examples), while the page itself would have to present a clear message (thesis) to the reader. With trained help on creating home pages using Internet software, teacher and students would become colearners in the process. Anyone who has ever collaborated on a writing project understands how important this metaphor can be.

▪ *There is no clear formula for writing the perfect paper, just as there is no clear formula for designing a perfect structure.* There are certain requirements for both, but creativity and originality, as well as audience, also have something to say in the matter! Whether we're talking about traditional forms like the five-paragraph theme or process writing that addresses real-world audiences, our students need some sense of how to meet their goals. Joan calls attention to the gap between the way students coming to college have been taught to write (or how they perceive they have been taught) and "how they need to write now."

Year after year, we hear the same question, "How long does it have to be?" when we give a writing assignment. We also deal in varying degrees with the issue of content versus form (mechanics of grammar, punctuation, sentence structure, spelling, and so on). Secondary teachers, like our college colleagues, face the same problems. Students who have never moved beyond traditional writing are not particularly strong writers. In many cases, teachers have provided the traditional model and that's what students tend to see as the *only* one that works. As more secondary teachers in other subjects value creativity in writing and thinking, students will become more adept at handling a variety of writing styles.

Students who are good writers must also learn to take risks with their writing and not settle for what is comfortable and easy. This year a senior I have known for several years came to the writing center to improve his writing. When I asked him why he was there, he said, "I know the formula for getting an A in English, but now I want to learn how to be a good writer." After I got up off the floor, I managed to reply, "Well, let's look at what you're doing and see how you can take some risks with your writing." He went on to spend a month working on a top-notch college essay that helped him with early decision at his favorite college. He has also written some colorful, exciting papers that resemble Joan's CVA metaphor!

■ *Joan offers some real classroom activities for the secondary level with the footprint ideas to begin discussions of writing.* As she states, "unless we bring students to an understanding of how they think about writing and about constructing texts, we will find it difficult to move them toward a more mature writing that exhibits critical thinking."

■ *Finally, as teachers we must be willing to try such collaborative efforts and to test the possibilities of using visual, concrete, tangible metaphors for teaching writing.* The ones Joan has offered enable writers to begin constructing texts that fulfill the purpose of the writer and the expectations of the reader.

Postscript

Joan makes a clear distinction between the traditional museum and the CVA as metaphors for traditional essays and for pieces that apply a complete writing process. I would like to go a step further. The purpose of the two structures differs. The old building is insular: the world is viewed through the art on the wall, so there is no need for windows. The new building, a visual arts center, focuses on teaching art by viewing the world through large windows. The structure is designed to open up space for creation and creativity.

We ought to talk less and draw more. I, personally, should like to renounce speech altogether and, like organic nature, communicate everything I have to say in sketches.
—JOHANN WOLFGANG VON GOETHE

Teaching Writing in a Visual Culture Across Disciplines

PAMELA B. CHILDERS

Over the years many of us have learned how to teach our own subject better by observing and listening to teachers in other disciplines. Through collaborative work and team teaching with colleagues across the secondary curriculum, I have discovered new approaches to learning. I am more aware of the importance of teaching writing in a visual culture since I have been seriously focused on the role of visuals in student learning. As my colleagues and I consider the purpose of writing assignments, we notice similar sensitivities to the relationship between visual images and written texts. Writing assignments in their courses also reflect this new awareness in both the writing prompts and the assessments. The following examples are from a variety of disciplines.

English as a Second Language

For many years, Catherine Neuhardt-Minor, an art teacher, and I have combined visuals and language to communicate with the exchange students who visit our school every year from a school in Japan. The students' stay is only three or four weeks, so their exposure to American English is limited. Our purpose is to enable students to create a symbolic vocabulary and translate it into a written language. We give students pieces of white paper and various writing implements (pens, felt tip markers, crayons), and demonstrate how to design marks for

Figure 5–1

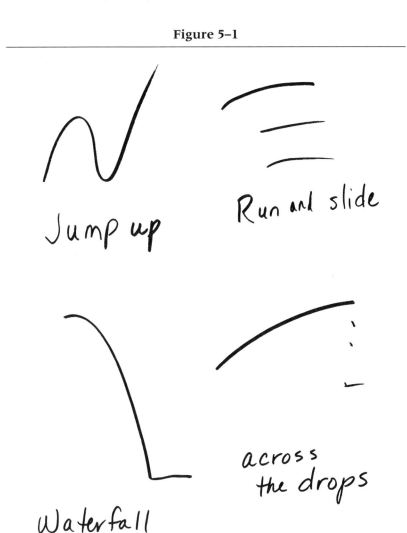

Jump up

Run and slide

Waterfall

across
the drops

the sounds they hear. Then we make a series of noises, usually high and low polysyllabic sounds that may be long or short in duration. Students sometimes laugh at the sounds, but since their language is so pictographic, it usually does not take them long to come up with beautiful, flowing marks to represent the sounds they hear. The class then shares their marks, and we encourage them to make the sounds that go with the marks. Now these marks become symbols, and after we model a few examples, we ask students to give words to their symbols. (See Figure 5–1.)

Sometimes the words are not English or any other familar language; at other times they may form a phrase inspired by the marks themselves. As long as the symbols and the words are meaningful to the writer, we encourage them to share their efforts. While we are all doing this exercise, the Japanese students are flipping frantically through their Japanese-English dictionaries to find the words they want. The students then write their words on the board, and we help rearrange and add to them by asking questions and getting input from other students. Finally, the students share their finished drafts. We hang them on the wall for all the Japanese exchange students and our American students to see. One year the students put the Japanese translation of their work beside the English version and (see Figure 5–2) gave it to us as a gift (it still hangs on the wall in the Caldwell Writing Center). This aural-visual-verbal collaborative exercise enables ESL students to communicate beyond language. Putting words to symbols that cannot be judged either correct or incorrect also enables the students to feel free to experiment in ways they wouldn't otherwise—and we all have fun learning together.

Art

Catherine Neuhardt-Minor has used many writing-to-learn activities with students in her art classes (see Neuhardt-Minor in *Programs and Practices*). The following two assignments involve a variety of ways of looking at visual images and interpreting the words of others through visual art.

Assignment One

In the first exercise students critically examine their own visual work, use appropriate vocabulary, and accurately portray the visual through language. Students write detailed descriptions of their own pencil drawing for a classmate to interpret visually with a new color drawing. They are asked to use as many elements (line, shape, value, texture, and so on) as possible and also encouraged to discuss scale, proportion, variety within unity, repetition, rhythm, balance, and directional forces. Their audience becomes real, and their purpose is to present a written description that can be interpreted visually.

In an assignment like this, students use verbal cues to convey the visual. They describe why they draw the way they do ("Instead of going for realistic shading, I shaded each surface . . . as if it were lighted by a separate, independent light source"), proportion and scale ("The hall seems to sail into perspective, with the corners of the wall going

Figure 5–2

In the summer Yoshino River with beautiful flowers that are blowing in the wind. The shadow of a flower in the bottom of the river is changing.

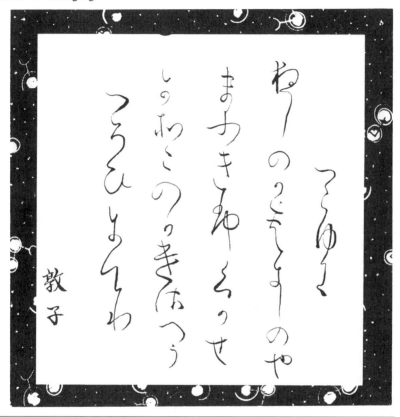

toward one point with the glass door at the end"), and variations on light and dark ("These puddles are generally gray in color, but the tone varies from puddle to puddle; the bottom puddle is slightly darker than the other two").

Assignment Two

The next assignment is an extension of the first. Students are asked to make a color drawing of the written description they have been given by their classmate. They may use any color medium available and are encouraged to do a great deal of thinking before they begin. They are also reminded that they are transposing a verbal description back into a spatial form. They also have to consider how they translate value (light and dark) to color.

This assignment again emphasizes language and the use of appropriate vocabulary to transfer meaning from writer to reader. In completing their own drawing, readers must interpret literally and figuratively the description they have been given. The first time an art teacher uses assignments like these, students may not understand the complexity of critical thinking or the creativity required to verbalize, comprehend, assimilate, and create. Notice also that in both assignments Catherine is judging not students' artistic ability but their critical thinking and their knowledge of the elements of art.

Science

Science is full of visual literacy. Every model, diagram, fetal pig, plant, or light optics computer program involves a visual and a verbal interpretation. Real-life examples like the tactile ones used in laboratory experiments or classroom activities, encourage students to put words to what they experience. Some of the assignments designed for specific science classes may be adapted for any of the sciences as well as for classes in any discipline.

Assignment One

In Peter LaRochelle's biology class, teams of students write descriptions and then create symbolic representations of the mechanism and orientation of active transport systems (sodium-potassium and proton pumps) on the mitochondrial membrane. Students develop an understanding of two active transport mechanisms through writing, cooperative learning, and peer evaluation. Then their understanding is evaluated through diagrammatic representations of written descriptions. Each team is given the name of one of the active transport systems. Students first write individually for ten minutes, then work collaboratively for five minutes to produce the best cooperative explanation possible. Teams exchange explanations with a group that has described the other active transport mechanism. Then, with three color markers and a large sheet of newsprint, each team is given fifteen minutes to draw the explanation they have received. When they have finished, the teams share their drawings with others by posting them around the room and describing them. This writing-to-learn activity enables students to review, rethink, and evaluate material they need to understand. Their individual written descriptions are evaluated as quiz grades and the best drawings are displayed in the hallway.

Students have learned the value of visual interpretation and verbal description. Months later, some students comment on the power of visual images in helping them to interpret material that they would previously have memorized and forgotten. They also mention how helpful it is to create metaphors that work for them; they may have learned less from their own group's efforts than from one of the other presentations hanging on the walls.

Assignment Two

In Michael Lowry's eighth-grade conceptual physical science class, students submit five portfolios during the school year. Four are used as formative assessment tools to focus on what and how students are learning, what the teacher may do to improve student learning, and how students see themselves as learners. The last portfolio is more reflective and functions as a summative assessment tool to determine what and how the students have learned, how they have grown as learners, and how the teacher has helped in each student's learning process. The unique aspect of this portfolio approach is that it combines visual and written communication in the learning process. The first requirement listed is "A visual (picture, diagram, drawing, etc.) and written description of a conceptual physics process. These should be pictures demonstrating 'physics in action.' Some of these will be used for classroom lessons" (Lowry 1996, 1).

To emphasize the relationship and importance of the visual in writing, the evaluation criteria include the quality of the portfolio: "The student demonstrates that he [or she] has taken time and applied his [or her] knowledge to superior written and visual responses to the assignments" (3). Further reinforcement of the value of the visual in the writing comes from multiple evaluations, one by the science teacher and one by the writing center director.

From these portfolios the teacher and writing center director have put together a list of student recommendations (Lowry and Childers 1997). On the first portfolios, students suggest

"Continue to work problems on the board to see how classmates work them out."

"Do more writing assignments that are short."

"Keeping a review journal isn't a bad idea."

"Visual creations as well as being told about things works well."

Once they become sensitive to the role of the visual in writing, young students respond with their own ideas about how important the visual is to writing and learning.

Assignment Three

In several biology classes, students complete a plant study and share their observations with peers, other students (younger and older), and adults (parents, teachers, members of the community). The biological study involves doing research and creating at least one image (photograph or artistic rendering) of four living plants in their own neighborhood or school environment. Each class prepares a class notebook that includes all the documentation organized and presented in a physical design agreed upon by the class. These notebooks are evaluated by external evaluators, and the winning notebook is then revised according to the evaluations and published for use in class presentations to younger students.

Students in each class have become very interested in the role the visual plays in the written presentation of information. Independently, classes have settled on entirely different designs. One class, for example, has decided that the visuals should be on the lefthand page and large enough to balance the written description on the righthand page. They feel that, since many students are more visually oriented, they would want to see what they are looking for in their own backyards and then read the text. Another class, in contrast, has insisted that the visuals should all be located at the back as an appendix so that the notebook forms two separate documents, a written one and a visual one. They claim that students trying to identify plants should have the visual representations grouped together so they can compare different plants in the notebook with the ones they are observing. The third class has chosen the direction most scientific books use—having pictures and text on the same page—because this offers more options for various learning styles. The amazing part of this design process is that students do much more thinking about content, audience, and purpose for the notebooks than they would without the inclusion of visuals. In addition, computers and the Internet have opened new visual areas.

History

In a sample lesson for history teachers this year, I gave an assignment that all can adapt to their own classes. The specific examples that I used were photographs from the Borneplatz in Frankfurt, Germany.

Figure 5–3
Road sign, Borneplatz, Frankfurt, Germany

I had taken a series of pictures of the cemetery marker describing the bombing of the synagogue at the beginning of World War II, the memorial sycamore trees around the symbolic block made with numbered stones from the remains of the synagogue, and the street signs in front of the memorial listing the various names of the Borneplatz and the years that it had been called each name (see Figure 5–3). As the last slide remains on the screen, I ask the history teachers to write a historical diary, journal entry, or letter reflecting some period in the life of this place. Since all have far greater knowledge than I of the historical events of World War II, I assure them that whatever they write will be a learning experience for me. They write for five or ten minutes. Afterwards, I notice the emotional impact of the photographs on what they have written. The image has permitted them to stray from the usual historical essay or research format. When I ask if they can use such an activity, most offer possibilities. They insist that photographs would offer them a chance to introduce a new historical period by having students write down their reactions, to review material students have previously covered as part of the prewriting for a written assignment, and to present a controversial issue for a persuasive essay.

Political cartoons that stimulate thinking and writing would also work extremely well. And who can ever forget the photojournalism of *Life* magazine during any major crisis? These exercises are far from fluff in history classes.

Here again, the Internet and CD technology offer added access to visual resources. The *Grolier Encyclopedia* CD-ROM, for instance, shows the footage of the Kennedy assassination, a Vietnam battle scene, and Maya Angelou reciting a poem at Clinton's inauguration. History comes alive and makes written response more concrete for our students when they have such visual triggers and connections.

Mathematics

I like the way visuals and writing work together in mathematics classes. In some cases the visual comes first, while in others the writing describes the visual the student must produce. The order depends on the purpose of the assignment. For instance, when a mathematics teacher wants students to learn specialized vocabulary for a particular mathematics course, he may have them try to describe a graph to a peer, who must then reproduce the graph from that written description alone. Students quickly see the need for appropriate terminology in talking about graphs (see Nickel 1994).

Assignment One

One way teachers of mathematics can apply visual awareness to writing is to have students write a letter home or to a younger student. In the letter, the students must describe a mathematical function using images to clarify the reader's understanding.

Assignment Two

In his geometry classes, David Perkinson uses the computer program Geometer's Sketchpad for writing-to-learn activities. Students visualize mathematical concepts and keep journals describing what they have done. As David describes it, "The writing exercises help me understand what aspects of the process need to be clarified further but also help the students move from (in Piaget's terms) the concrete operational stage to the formal operational stage" (Perkinson, 23). In this way, David thinks "students can connect the concrete application of the mathematical skills to the abstract understanding of the mathematical concepts." As he experiments with using visuals to teach writing in mathematics, David concludes, "Visual activities naturally provide a context for the study of the concepts, and the use of writing exercises enables the students to move from a superficial memorization of skills to a deeper understanding of abstract concepts" (24).

English and Other Areas

As an English teacher, I want to be sure to mention an activity that my colleagues Cleve Latham and Hank Hopping added to their junior English classes last year. In his introduction to Walt Whitman, Cleve gave students a demonstration of how to use the computer program PowerPoint to present written information in a visual format. Then he and Hank asked students to select an American writer and prepare a visual/written presentation emphasizing key points about the writer and his or her writings. Students spent time doing research in books and on the Internet to get information they wished to include in their written presentation using the appropriate visuals. Yes, some presentations did not demonstrate great writing, thinking, or use of visuals, but there were also a few that benefitted the entire class. The students also learned to write concisely in order to fit the key information into the PowerPoint format. Josh, for instance, gave a presentation on horror fiction that demonstrated all the appropriate techniques of both a good essay and a good speech. This kind of assignment certainly has a place in the English class to help students organize their thoughts and present them in an appropriate manner.

In addition to these few examples of teaching writing in a visual culture across disciplines, other subject areas such as foreign languages and music should not be overlooked. Each offers rich resources of teaching writing. One foreign language teacher I know uses cartoons with empty bubbles in each frame. Students fill in the bubbles with the dialogue in that language, demonstrating their interpretive knowledge of visual images, then translating that into speech.

In teaching music, set aside music videos and instead consider how music is *composed* on a computer. Because the computer supplies visual images of sounds, it is possible to add lyrics within an ever-changing format. I have watched my stepchildren move sounds on the monitor into the correct position for timing, melody, and lyrics to work together. They are "reading" what they are creating with visuals, sound, and words.

In gender issues and human development classes, photographs and works of art are useful in stimulating writing about human interactions. Stereotypes, inappropriate actions, and moral issues are clarified when students have the opportunity to visualize and then verbalize their reactions. With some ingenuity, a little thought, and consideration of the variety of learning styles in any classroom, teachers may realize the importance of connecting the visual with writing as a means of discovery, renewal, organization, focus, review, and evaluation.

Response

ERIC H. HOBSON

I n this chapter, Pam has accomplished two important tasks—one overt, one implicit:

- She has catalogued a number of ways in which teachers success-fully integrate visual-verbal pedagogy into their courses across disciplines. And, in doing so, she demonstrates that these teachers have not encountered (or, at least, not been hogtied by) the dreaded loss of "content" coverage that many teachers assume re-sults from any class activity other than a lecture.

- Through these snippets of classroom application, Pam provides a powerful model of how a writing-across-the-curriculum (WAC) program can be established without waging a continuous cam-paign of hard-sell tactics, shame, and administrative pressure along with the perpetual twisting of volunteer faculty arms. This chapter highlights the ease with which writing and visual activi-ties intersect in many different disciplinary settings to help meet the pedagogical situations and needs unique to these knowledge communities. And by working with faculty to make the most of this opportunity, Pam is afforded a unique chance to help instill writing as a centerpiece of students' learning, regardless of each course's discipline-specific peculiarities.

Reflection

As someone who has been both a faculty developer and a coordinator of writing across the curriculum, I too have experienced the payoff I attribute to Pam's cross-curricular partnerships in terms of increased ease of access to disciplinary classrooms and faculty. In particular, I found that faculty in the biological sciences have long used drawing as a tool for helping students learn about the interior and exterior organic world. In biology and physiology labs, for example, students draw pictures of, among other things, cellular structure and activity as witnessed through the microscope, and pictures of the skeletal, muscular, and organ systems of any number of animals, themselves included. The extent of their drawing is impressive. Likewise, I am impressed and, admittedly, somewhat befuddled by the fact that students don't seem to resist the requirement to draw in the same manner, and with the same vigor, they do the requirement to write. Even if students don't think of themselves as good at drawing, they will still give it their best shot in the lab. As a biology colleague once explained to me over coffee, "I find that in drawing biological systems at the level of the cellular system and the organ system, students show me what they know and don't know. Their drawings are quite revealing. Often parts of the whole are completely out of whack proportionally, reflecting the student's unbalanced understanding of the total process or system—they know the parts, but not the whole."

The problem with the activity from my collegue's perspective was that drawing, while extremely useful in and of itself, didn't take the students far enough in terms of helping them master the material. While the students almost always got their drawings to represent cell, organs, bones, and so on accurately, that level of control over the material did not ensure that the students could articulate their understanding in writing—when it came time for the test, they could draw the item requested but had a hard time writing about their new knowledge.

Like Pam, I used this concern about students' active learning as an opportunity to introduce written tasks to the drawing activities, ostensibly to help students prepare for exams. Doing so required that I sit down with the biology and physiology faculty members to discuss specific assignments and how they might fit into the lab work as well as the overall course design. The resulting discussion of course goals and desired student outcomes was enlightening for everyone involved. The faculty came away with class/lab/exam activities that helped to move students to the desired level of understanding and articulation; I gained WAC colleagues without coercion. Everyone was pleased.

Thematic Variation

In keeping with Pam's WAC focus, I want to suggest an additional activity that can find a home in the course activities notebook in any number of disciplines. A common assignment given in technical writing courses asks students to study a tool or a process and produce the instruction/procedures documents necessary for someone (usually a lay person) to use the tool or follow the process to its completion successfully. Without a doubt, there is value in having students engage in the type of close observation of detail needed to provide a reader with the requisite instruction for carrying out the task. When presented at this level, however, the activity is contrived. As a result, students get bored and complain, with some merit, that it doesn't reflect "real world" situations.

In an effort to engage students in the task of observing closely and trying to predict the problems another person might face in using a tool or following a process, many instructors add a more tactile, hands-on element to the assignment by having students construct the items they then describe. The operative logic here is intuitive: The builder is more familiar with an item than anyone else and should be the person best suited to describe it to the people who will use it.

My favorite example of this extension of the task is that of a colleague who teaches technical writing. Her students use Tinkertoys to construct an apparatus able to complete a specific task as determined by its creators. What emerges from the team's planning and building sessions often multicolored, rubberband-driven, Rube Goldbergesque contraptions intended to do things like turn a book's page, walk completed papers to the teacher's desk, rotate on a central axis, and other equally zany (and useless) tasks. But what also emerges are excited and engaged students who, in the process of writing instruction manuals, often discover that they have designed logistical nightmares. Usually the apparatus seems deceptively simple to document, until the team actually tries to recount the entire building process so that another team can successfully construct it. And usually the documents the teams write get down to specific details and provide users with the information they need. However, these instructions often have informational and procedural holes that cause their beta testers enormous headaches and send their authors back to revision sessions. More often than not, the instructions lack visual aids to provide readers with additional information about how the apparatus is constructed and what activity it performs. They assume that the users of the apparatus solve problems best by reading about them. A central tenet of technical communication, however, is that most readers benefit enormously from visually rich texts.

The Next Step, Drawing . . .

When required to provide visual representations of their apparatus, many groups produce flat, two-dimensional pictures that give a general overview of the object at best. These renderings relay little sense of the complexity of the object's design, nor, on a more mundane level, do they supply details on exactly where and how the Tinkertoy poles, wheels, and plastic fins join. In other words, the pictures do not provide much useful information for replicating the apparatus.

When required to produce a series of study sketches of the object (front, side, and top views; negative space studies; exploded views; extreme close-ups), however, the construction teams usually make important discoveries:

- "exploded" views of the object can serve in place of many repetitive steps in the construction directions
- close-up images help illustrate intricate relationships and construction steps particularly well
- studies from different angles can help predict where problems in replicating the apparatus will likely arise

With this increased understanding of their apparatus, the members of the design team are better prepared to revise their instruction manual for greater efficiency, audience accommodation, and use of visual materials. Frequently, the drawings made during this stage of the project do not appear in the final document; rather, they serve solely as discovery and problem-solving tools, in much the same manner in which architects, engineers, and artists use them (see Graves 1977; Chapter 8).

. . . Then Writing

An additional layer is added to this activity by encouraging students to write (informally), either when they take a break from drawing their object or immediately after they have finished their sketches. Useful writing prompts for this stage of discovery and reflection can be as simple as, "While drawing, what did you notice about your apparatus for the first time? Is this important?" Or, following group comparisons and discussion of the sketches, prompts can encourage students to reflect on the project's progress to date and to plan for the next stage of revision.

Back to WAC

Adding a layer of informal drawing-as-problem-solving to complex projects, such as the Tinkertoy project described above, provides students with heuristics for rethinking their preconceptions about the task at hand, for achieving a measure of critical distance, and for considering the needs of their intended audience. All of these are benefits that accrue to students in similar rhetorical situations in many disciplinary settings. For example, students in organic chemistry classes and labs are frequently required to draw molecular structures for the compounds they are studying. Their tendency to represent these structures in flat two-dimensional ways limits their understanding of how the structures affect and determine the actions and reactions that these compounds can cause and participate in. Adding informal drawing activities that require students to explore (in teams or individually) these chemical structures from a variety of visual perspectives provides them with more information about the interrelationship between molecular form and function. Informal, short writes and quick reflective notes are a natural partner to these drawing activities and provide writing faculty a convenient entry point for collaboration with their colleagues in the natural sciences.

Postscript

While often daunting, creating cross-curricular links is worth the effort, especially in terms of benefits to student learning and faculty cooperation. Yet, making connections across the curriculum through a focus on student writing may not always be the best approach for forming the relationships necessary to implement writing across the curriculum. As I have found in my efforts to get my writing agenda's metaphoric foot in the door of many disciplines, starting with the visual pedagogical tools that disciplines such as biology and chemistry routinely use has been effective. I ask questions about what helps students learn most effectively in these areas. I listen to my colleagues' responses and their usual segues into what students "still do not get" using these methods. Then, and only then, do I talk about how I address the same issues in writing classes and suggest that if by combining their visual strategies for the sciences and my verbal teaching strategies for writing we might create a more effective tool at our collective disposal.

The aim of every artist is to arrest motion, which is life, by artificial means and hold it fixed so that one hundred years later when a stranger looks at it, it moves again since it is life.
—WILLIAM FAULKNER

The Civil War and Its Monuments
Visualizing the Past

RICHARD H. PUTNEY

The apparent gaps between visual and verbal expression can effectively be bridged through interdisciplinary projects that combine writing and visualization. As evidence I offer the experience of a writing-across-the-curriculum (WAC) course, "Hallowed Ground: Monuments, Memory and the American Civil War," which I team taught in the spring of 1994. As an associate professor of art history, I was fortunate to have Tom Lingeman, an associate professor of sculpture, as an outstanding collaborator. The course Tom and I gave to undergraduate students used Civil War monuments to achieve an essential goal: that course members understand and appreciate the design, production, and meaning of such memorial sculptures in their historical context. By combining the visual and the verbal, the course gave students multiple ways to internalize what they read and saw—and it enabled them to objectify what was so much a part of their own cultural history. Tom and I wanted students to learn effectively and meaningfully about how the Civil War motivated memorial activities, both verbal and visual; the latter, of course, included the delivery of memorial orations, the writing and publication of literary texts, and the design and production of tangible monuments of granite, marble, and bronze.

Allied with this goal was the desire to have students experience how images and words express powerful ideas and emotions.

Monuments were perfect for such an exercise, because their interpretation required the study of both texts and images. More important, the monuments themselves combined text and image.
Nineteenth-century artisans gave them forms powerfully charged
with traditional associations, embellished them with inscriptions,
and quite often enlivened them with images. Thus, form, image,
and word were combined to convey specific historical and cultural
messages; moreover, at dedication ceremonies, spoken words en-
dowed monuments with commemorative life. Without question,
Civil War monuments provided wonderful material for a course
devoted to the exploration of verbal and visual expression within
that historical period.

To achieve these objectives we had the students read, analyze,
and discuss various primary and secondary texts associated with one
of the war's most famous battles, Gettysburg, and to supplement the
reading with palpable experiences of memorial landscapes and monuments, especially those at Gettysburg National Military Park. Even
more significant was the fact that the students themselves, working in
groups, designed and fabricated actual monuments. Such activities,
supplemented by a rigorous round of journal assignments, gave each
member of the course an intense and immediate encounter with an
important event and with the literary and artistic means by which it
was preserved in historic memory. Key to the course's structure was
its unusual emphasis on combining reading, discussion, writing,
sketching, study in the field, and hands-on work in the sculpture studio. Highly experimental, the course required an unusual level of
faculty collaboration and a surprisingly unusual approach to interdisciplinary teaching in the fine arts.

Faculty Collaboration:
Different Disciplines, A Shared Passion

Faculty collaboration was key to the course's success. Tom is a very
talented sculptor who specializes in abstract works cast in bronze,
and he is very much a part of the contemporary art scene. I'm an art
historian whose specialty is the interpretation of medieval images.
Neither of us has had much formal training in the history of the
Civil War; however, both of us have read widely on American art
and history, and have pursued a keen interest in the history of monuments. Indeed, in a casual discussion in 1991, Tom and I discovered
our mutual passion for the sculptures at Gettysburg; I had been sys-
tematically photographing them, and Tom had been analyzing their
materials and techniques with a sculptor's well-trained eye.

Integrating the Visual and the Verbal:
An Unusual Interdisciplinary Approach

Because they share an interest in the visual arts, studio fine arts and
art history might seem indistinguishable in the minds of most acade-
mics. But just ask art historians or studio artists—or their students!—
about the relationship of the two disciplines. Just as composition or
math students might resent drawing or visual strategies in the classroom, so, too, studio majors think they have escaped verbal expression. However, as experience shows, the visual artist must rely on the
intellect just as the historian makes use of verbal expression. Similarly, the art historian depends on a highly developed sense of visual
perception, and, like the artist, is often driven by emotional, aesthetic,
or spiritual needs.

In spite of their keen interest in the visual arts, however, students
in art history sometimes resemble majors in other, less visually oriented concentrations such as English. Often they are fearful or dis-
dainful of courses in the studio fine arts. They are afraid to test their
own aptitudes in terms of hands-on visual expression, or, sadly, they
feel that visual and manual skills are trivial compared to verbal ones.
On the other hand, studio majors sometimes distrust art history
courses, fearing that they will be entrapped in a useless, irrelevant
past, be "forced to live in books," or have their expression confined to
the merely verbal. These interdisciplinary tensions in the visual arts
reflect similar tensions between other academic disciplines, and they
are but a single manifestation of a dichotomy endemic in the western
cultural tradition: *the visual and physical are often set in opposition and
subjugated to the verbal and intellectual.* Therefore, although what is described here was developed for interdisciplinary teaching in the visual
arts, many of the instructional techniques used also apply to teaching
in other disciplines.

Planning an Interdisciplinary Course

Like many professors, Tom and I like to talk a lot, and we worried that
this might get in the way of the *collective* planning of the course. To
avoid this potential problem we used a planning tactic derived from
our experiences in teaching other WAC courses. Working at the same
table, each of us wrote informally in a journal about the course goals
and the methods to be used in achieving them. When we had finished
writing, we read our entries aloud to one another. This method
worked well for us because it gave free rein to the brainstorming
needed for effective course planning, made each of us listen carefully

to the other's ideas, and gave each of us the floor to present our own. The result was an innovative and effective course plan that synthesized the best ideas from each of us.

Overview of the Course: A Sentimental and Romantic Drama in Three Acts

The eleven-week, quarter-long course was to have three parts. Since the monuments at Gettysburg were driven by the experience of war, the first part, (meant to last two-and-a-half weeks on the quarter system) was devoted to the experience of the Civil War itself; it moved from generalizations about wartime experiences to more focused aspects of the Gettysburg campaign. This portion of the course took place in small classrooms in the art department and made use of texts, images, and artifacts.

The next phase of the course focused on monuments and memorial activities. Although the fighting of a Civil War battle and the placement of monuments on the site are related events, they are also quite distinct. As Tom and I told our students, the soldiers did not carry bronze or granite monuments with them into battle, setting them in place as soon as gunfire had ceased. The Battle of Gettysburg occurred over three days (July 1–3, 1863), and memorialization of the site began quite soon with the dedication of the National Cemetery in November 1863. But only a handful of monuments were erected on the battlefield in the next two decades, and the vast majority of the more than five hundred currently there were dedicated only in the late 1880s and 1890s. Thus, in the second part of the course, our focus was to move from the 1860s to the late 1880s. This phase, lasting a week and a half, was devoted to memorial activities in general, and to the production of monuments in particular. Again we made use of assigned readings, images, and classroom discussion, but we also increased our use of visualization and made field trips to appropriate sites, culminating in a four-day field trip to Gettysburg intended to synthesize all the material covered in the first month.

The third and last portion of the course was the lengthiest and the most intense. The students divided up into small teams and assumed historical roles. Each group represented an association of veterans and artists working in the year 1888, and each was charged with memorializing a single regiment's participation in the Battle of Gettysburg. Specifically, the group members designed and cast a bronze model of a monument for their regiment, wrote the monument's inscriptions, developed a site plan for its placement on the Gettysburg battlefield, wrote a brief history of the unit's participation in the battle, and composed a speech to be delivered at the monument's dedicatory ceremony. We set aside the last class session—normally reserved for a final examination—for monument dedication ceremonies.

Act I: The Experience of the Civil War

As instructors, our primary purpose was less to impart knowledge to our students than to motivate them to seek it out for themselves. We wanted, above all, to engage students both intellectually and emotionally, and we wanted them to know the class was theirs, not ours. We tried our best to avoid inserting our own values or conclusions into discussions, acting instead as facilitators and moderators.

Our class was limited to fourteen students we had specially recruited for this first attempt at the course. Evenly distributed in terms of gender, six were majors in art history, seven in studio art, and one a double major; only four had previous experience in sculpture. To warm our students to the subject matter, we opened the first course session with a "light and sound show." In a darkened room, with only a brief welcome from Tom and me, we played the first two movements of Dvořák's *American Quartet.* As accompaniment to that exquisite piece, we projected dozens of slides depicting the landscape at Gettysburg and a number of the monuments dedicated there during the 1880s and 1890s. For many of us it was an evocative and powerful experience; both Tom and I got a gut feeling that it engaged students' interest from the start. Shifting from the visual and aural to the verbal, we distributed the first informal writing assignment for the course journal. Entitled "The Civil War and You," it asked students to write informally for about twenty minutes on their own feelings about the Civil War.

Once all of us had finished writing, we went around the room. Students introduced themselves and briefly discussed their majors, career goals, and interest in the course subject matter. We then opened the floor to the issues involved in the assignment. Students were hesitant for only a few moments. The lengthy discussion that ensued involved almost everyone in the class and touched on many vital issues, including slavery, pacifism, notions of masculinity, and the essence of the American experience. We learned that one student was a Civil War buff and that several others had ancestors who fought in the war. Also obvious was a nearly universal bias against the Confederacy and some deep divisions over the morality of war (which would become even more visceral during the second class session).

Reversing the usual order of a course, we finished the first day's session by distributing the syllabus, which, like the course, mixed text and image; after going over the course goals and assignments, we gave students their first reading assignments: Michael Shaara's Pulitzer Prize-winning novel about the Battle of Gettysburg, *The Killer Angels*, which they were to finish in a week, and Shelby Foote's highly praised account of the battle, "Stars in Their Courses" (1974).

For the second class session, we opened with a journal assignment, intended to provoke contemplation and discussion of the experience of the war, which emphasized the important role played by the imagination in the reconstruction of the past. Asking students to imagine what the war experience might have been like, we gave them the option of assuming the identity of a Civil War soldier; about half did so, and one class member wrote her journal entry in the form of a soldier's letter.

We had originally planned to have a group discussion of this journal topic and to follow it with our only formal lecture in the course, an overview of the Civil War experience of the ordinary soldier based upon the interpretation of drawings, paintings, and photographs from the period. But Tom had a great idea for supplementing and invigorating the lecture. Borrowing a local collector's Civil War arms and accoutrements, he brought them to class; after the group discussion we brought the objects out, explained them, and encouraged students to handle them. This proved to be a fascinating and catalytic experience! There was bit of posturing and affected nonchalance on the part of some students and a good deal of horror on the part of others. Whatever the reaction, the objects—a Springfield rifle with fixed bayonet, for example—made it easy to appreciate the truly lethal nature of the Civil War. Such an experience not only deepened the impact of the lecture that followed, it would prove very useful to a fuller understanding of the assigned readings. Most gratifying was the student conversation on the nature and validity of war, which the writing assignment and the objects provoked. Despite their widely divergent opinions, the students treated one another with great sensitivity and respect.

For the next session we moved to a small seminar room to begin discussions of the assigned texts. The first was devoted to *The Killer Angels*, a book we chose because it presents numerous dramatic situations and fascinating characters in lively prose; moreover, it conveys an essentially accurate, engaging, and nearly unforgettable account of the battle's history. We devised two journal assignments to get at some important aspects of the text: narrative, point of view, structure, character development, and the nature of historicity. The assignments also were intended to stimulate discussion of the book during the second week of the course.

To put it mildly, student response to the book was enthusiastic; Tom and I hardly had to say a thing in our first two-hour discussion. People waxed poetic, argued about the author's point of view, and contemplated the fate of the characters. Their favorite, incidentally, was Joshua Chamberlain, commanding officer of the 20th Maine Volunteers, whose regiment's action on the second day's battle played a major role in Shaara's narrative. This journal entry was typical: "My favorite episode . . . was Chamberlain's defense of Little Round Top. All the noise, confusion, terror and exhilaration of battle were brilliantly portrayed, plus a victory against seemingly hopeless odds is always satisfying—especially when victory comes from brilliant leadership."

We concluded our study of Shaara with an exercise involving visualization. To reinforce their appreciation of space, we asked class members to draw maps of the Gettysburg region without consulting the maps in Shaara's book. Not surprisingly, given the enthusiasm for Shaara, most of the drawings were accurate and useful; for those that weren't, a conversation with their classmates helped students understand why they weren't.

For the next session we read Shelby Foote's account of the battle. His text is a traditional historical narrative but, like Shaara's, it is also beautifully written, engaging, and informative; it also gives a more comprehensive view of the battle of Gettysburg than does *The Killer Angels*. There are many other accounts of the three-day battle, some far too lengthy for our course, others very dry or highly technical. Foote gave us the historical and spatial overview we needed, but he did so in a way that caught the mood of flesh and blood people acting out a drama on a very large stage. We devised a writing assignment to complement this reading that was similar to that for *The Killer Angels*. This too inspired good discussion about the nature and relationship of literature and history, as this student response demonstrates: "The narrator [of Foote's text] is *not* a participant in the battle on either side. While Shaara would at times move into someone's mind and allow the thoughts and feelings of the character to tell the story, Foote remains outside of the characters in the third-person, describing actions in a consistent manner which, while not as enthralling as Shaara's presentation, nevertheless is effective in aiding the reader's understanding of people and events."

We concluded our discussion of Foote's account with a verbal word game on narrative history. I began the game with a single sentence on the development of the Gettysburg campaign (something like: "On the morning of July 1, 1863, John Buford's cavalry confronted Confederate infantry northwest of the town of Gettysburg"). Going around our seminar table in turn, each person was to continue the story with a single sentence describing the unfolding of events in time and space. Usually it went quickly and smoothly, but at times it was interrupted by outbreaks of dissent. One student's sentence might invoke the mock wrath of other class members ("But you forgot so-and-so. . . ." "No! that came later. . . .") and the temporary halt would lead to a new start. It was engaging and fun, and taught us a lot about the construction of narrative—a spatial skill.

Act II: Commemorating the War

We began the second phase of the course by turning from the history of the battle of Gettysburg to American attitudes and traditions about it. In a single week we were able to accomplish a great deal, and this through a rich conjunction of reading, discussion, visualization, and study in the field. First we read portions of Garry Wills' *Lincoln at Gettysburg*, complementing the book's acute and moving analysis of early memorial activities at Gettysburg with on-site studies of local monuments and their settings. Our goal was to better understand how the production of Civil War monuments participated in and was informed by larger social and cultural forces. The first two chapters in *Lincoln at Gettysburg* concern themselves with precisely this issue: how the words spoken by Lincoln and Edward Everett at the dedication of the National Cemetery at Gettysburg in November 1863 commemorated the Union sacrifice, and why the enunciation of those words in a specific physical setting—a cemetery—had rich associations for members of American society in the nineteenth-century.

In reading Wills—and the words of Lincoln and Everett—our students explored the attitudes and values that would lead Americans to sponsor, design, and produce an enormous number of monuments to commemorate the war. To understand the forms such monuments would take, we followed our reading of Wills with site visits to memorial landscapes in the Toledo area. The most important of these was Woodlawn, a cemetery begun in the 1870s and located in the northern regions of the city. Tom and I had devised two assignments for the site and, on an appropriately gloomy morning, our group paid a visit. In a light drizzle we wandered, journals and clipboards in hand, through its green, parklike setting. There we followed winding roads and paths, exploring a landscape of ponds, meadows, and gently rolling ridges. All was carefully planted with flowers, shrubs, and large, venerable trees. Throughout, the landscape was marked with monuments of granite, marble, and bronze. What we encountered at Woodlawn, of course, was a product of the "rural cemetery" movement. Extremely characteristic of the nineteenth century, such a landscape was one of the purest expressions of Romanticism's evocative association of nature, history, memory, and death. Woodlawn that morning provided our students with a palpable experience of the previous century's use of memorial environments and specific monumental forms. Used before the war to mark the graves of individuals, in the decades following the conflict such monuments would be adapted for use as war memorials for urban squares and the more rural landscapes of Civil War battlefields.

Our first assignment asked students to wander alone through the cemetery to explore the essential nature of Woodlawn and to sketch and describe its environment. We concluded our visit with a "scavenger hunt" in one relatively confined section of the cemetery. There, class members were to seek out and draw specific iconographic motifs that Tom and I had discovered on an earlier scouting expedition: sculptural representations of a sleeping lamb, for example, a boulder, a cherub, a sphere, a wreath, and a tree stump. Sketching, like free writing in a journal, is a marvelous aid to learning; even if students have little or no talent for reproducing what they see, the drawing will sharpen their observation, understanding, and recollection. The specific objective in this exercise was to make associations between the expression of themes in memorial texts (introduced in Wills) and the visual motifs in the cemetery to integrate verbal and visual expression.

To complete this day's journey to the nineteenth century we engaged in the personal, the sentimental, and the imaginary. Selecting particularly engaging individual or family monuments, the students were to compose imaginary stories about them as soon as possible after leaving the cemetery; here they used inscriptions and sculptural motifs to inspire literary productions.

For our other local field trip, we visited Johnson's Island located along the shore of Lake Erie. Used as a prison camp for captured Confederate officers during the war, the site today includes a fine bronze and granite monument to those who died in captivity dedicated in 1906. We had everyone sketch the monument and record its inscriptions; what followed was a lively group discussion of the monument's iconography.

Having completed the initial reading and field trips, students already possessed a good general knowledge of the battle of Gettysburg and a good introduction to nineteenth-century monuments. They were ready to conclude this second part of the course with an experience of the Gettysburg site. Early on a Thursday morning in late April, we piled into cars and vans, and drove the 400 miles to eastern Pennsylvania.

Our visit provided vivid experiences for all of us, many focusing

Figure 6–1
Monument to General Warren (1888), Little Round Top,
Gettysburg National Military Park

on the evocative relationship of monument and landscape. At times we gathered the entire class at sites of great significance to the course of the battle or at monuments of particular interest. Driving through the dying light of sunset one evening, for example, we parked near the top of Little Round Top, climbed its eastern slope, and passed over the crest to gather around the bronze statue of General Gouverneur K. Warren (see Figure 6–1). Sharing his high vantage point, we encountered a receding vista of rolling ridges cut by dark lines of trees. The dramatic siting made it easy to imagine what Warren had seen and felt during the battle. Indeed, the abstraction of a battlefield map, its topography reduced to contour lines and its regiments of soldiers to

Figure 6–2
Sherri Simon sketches the monument of the 116th Pennsylvania
Infantry (1889), the Loop, Gettysburg National Military Park

rectangles, took on a more immediate meaning that was impossible to forget. It was also clear why it had been so important to commemorate Warren's foresight and decisiveness with a well-placed monument.

Another memorable group experience was a presentation on Cemetery Ridge given by Scott Hartwig, an articulate young park historian. Scott spoke to us before a granite obelisk erected in honor of the 69th Pennsylvania Volunteers, a regiment that suffered the brunt of Pickett's Charge on the final day of battle. He cleverly positioned our group so we looked out over a low stone wall, the regiment's only substantial line of defense, to the open fields crossed by Pickett's men in their final assault. The impact of the setting helped us imagine the horrific culmination of the battle. At first summarizing aspects of the regiment's early history, Scott then turned to its fearful experiences on July 3, 1863. Citing from memory the letters and journals of soldiers who had occupied the line of battle that day, Scott delivered an account that was inspiring, at times grisly, and impossible to forget. It was easy to relate to the soldiers of the 69th Pennsylvania, not as mythic heroes, but as ordinary people who had experienced the extraordinary.

Equally as affecting as these group experiences was the work the students did on their own. Our primary assignments for Gettysburg called for the students to commune individually with the monuments that appealed to them; thus, we asked each one to spend a full day exploring favorite portions of the battlefield, writing general descriptions of at least three monuments and recording their inscriptions, and sketching their images in course journals (Figure 6–2). Our work complete, we left for home the following morning.

Act III: Creating Monuments

Every assignment and course experience, from the opening slide show through the trip to Gettysburg, served as preparation for what followed: six weeks devoted to the design and fabrication of hypothetical monuments for specific sites at Gettysburg. Everyone knew the story of the battle, was well acquainted with the site and its monuments, and was highly motivated to face the course's most difficult challenge. At the beginning of the fifth week, Tom and I divided students into teams, assigned each a Civil War regiment, and distributed instructions for the final course projects.

It was a challenge to divide the students into effective design teams. Because of our classroom discussions, field trips, and shared rooms and meals, everyone knew everyone else, so we didn't have much to guess about in terms of who got along (most did) and who didn't. What was critical, however, was how each group decided to distribute the work on their group assignments. Each team was to act as the monument committee for a single unit that fought at Gettysburg, to design its monument, write its inscriptions, and fabricate a small preliminary model, or maquette, in bronze. It was also to compose a unit history, devise a site plan, and write a dedicatory oration. To help in assembling effective groups, we surveyed class members about what types of activities most interested them (writing, research, drawing or sculpting, for example) and what skills they felt they brought to the table. Tom and I assigned them to teams based upon their responses; obviously, we made sure we didn't have all sculptors in one group and all writers or researchers in another. Although there was to be some division of labor in each group—some would specialize in drawing, molding clay, or writing—we wanted everyone to participate in the creation of all the group's products: monument sketches and maquettes, texts, and site plans.

But how could everyone participate in creating such a diverse range of products requiring such a diverse range of skills? In the late nineteenth century, monuments commemorating the Civil War were the products of very similar collaborative efforts; artists and craftsmen *made* them, but they worked with committees of veterans, politicians, and officials to arrive at final designs. We asked our students to contribute to their team efforts in the same way; although everyone was to have particular responsibility for one of the team creations, or to be relied upon for one type of skill or activity, each was to make some contribution to the final appearance or content of everything the group produced.

One of the most exciting moments of this class session occurred during the group selection of Civil War units. We asked each team member to write down the type of unit for which they would like to create a monument—Union or Confederate, for example, and infantry, cavalry, or artillery. It was quickly decided that everyone wanted to represent a Union infantry regiment, and that the 20th Maine, the 69th Pennsylvania, and the 6th Wisconsin were all highly desirable choices. The names of these three were placed in a hat (appropriately, a blue Union kepi) and we had a drawing. There was loud cheering as the group that went first had the good fortune to pick the class favorite, Colonel Joshua Chamberlain's 20th Maine Regiment, the heroes of Little Round Top. Fortunately the other groups were happy with their picks too, and we turned at last to the distribution and discussion of the final assignments.

An important hypothetical assumption for the final project was that none of the regimental monuments that today grace the battle-field had yet been put in place; the students had to imagine that they were designing for a site as yet unmarked. Each group was to design its monument in a style appropriate to the year 1888, the twenty-fifth anniversary of the battle, which meant that the design had to be in accordance with the regulations of the Gettysburg Battlefield Memorial Association, a private association of citizens and veterans that administered the battlefield from 1864 to 1895. The students were given copies of the Association's regulations governing aspects of a monument's design, including its materials ("of granite or real bronze"), the size, quality, and content of its inscriptions ("letters not less than four inches long . . . deeply and distinctly cut . . . with a brief statement of any important movement [the unit] made") and its siting ("on the line of battle . . . [with any] statue or figure of a soldier [facing] the enemy's line"). Assignments in hand, we left the classroom for the last time and headed for Tom's sculpture studio. The most important and exciting phase of the course was about to begin.

On the first day in the studio, Tom introduced students to its layout, its facilities, and any safety hazards. He then gave a brief overview of the various techniques and processes essential to the fabrication of a bronze sculpture. When we set the groups loose to develop their designs and to divide up their essential tasks, each took a work space in the studio and began deliberations.

The next week was characterized by organized chaos. Students al-

Figure 6–3
The 20th Maine group forms a mold around their
clay image of Col. Joshua Chamberlain

ternately talked quietly, argued, laughed, yelled, ran to the library, sketched, pouted, or wrote in their journals. Surprisingly quickly, they developed both their group rapport and a sophisticated and highly plausible design for a monument. As we had hoped, each member provided input on the group's monument design.

Finishing their designs on paper in a week and a half, the students submitted them to Tom and me acting as the board of the Gettysburg Battlefield Memorial Association. We made suggestions and granted final approval; both of us gave consideration to historic plausibility and aesthetics, while Tom made important technical suggestions. Happily, only minor changes were necessary, and the monument designs were

Figure 6–4

Molten bronze enters a mold made by the 69th Pennsylvania group

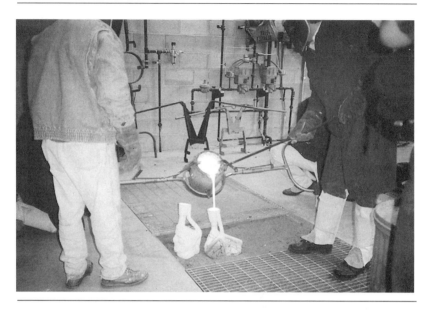

ready to be transformed from works on paper to more substantial objects. Tom demonstrated the processes for making prototypes in temporary materials like clay, wood, and wax, and for making the molds
necessary for the production of the final bronze sculpture. Well-
guided by Tom and the team members who were sculpture majors,
every single student participated in the physical construction of the
prototypes and molds (Figure 6–3); most had never before set foot in
a studio. The atmosphere in the studio was intense and—except for
the repeated playing of the soundtrack from Ken Burns' PBS docu-
mentary on the Civil War—very quiet. Tom and I made suggestions
throughout, but students mostly worked in their own groups. Dedicated to the task at hand, most put in extra hours outside class time,
especially in the evenings.

As the temporary models in wood, clay and wax neared completion, Tom demonstrated how we would render them in bronze. He
taught us how to make molds that would retain the form and detail of
our prototypes but also withstand the rigors of the molten metal.
Looking like owls in their respirators, students worked with Tom to
make strong silica shell molds reinforced by steel wire; a well-con-
structed mold would give each group a single chance.

Once the molds were finished, we were ready for a training ses-

Figure 6–5
Monument of the 6th Wisconsin group

sion on the most exciting step in the process of fabricating a bronze sculpture—pouring molten bronze. As they watched the glowing yellow metal flow into molds, students felt challenged, even a little scared. (I sure did!) But Tom was reassuring, demonstrating that what seemed complex was the result of a careful sequence of relatively simple processes. Like a good coach he gave us all the inspiration and knowledge we needed to succeed—and we did!

Finally the day came when each group would "do the pour" for its own sculpture. It began early one morning as a gas furnace melted bronze ingots in a heavy crucible; meanwhile, the just-finished molds were carefully arranged in sand in a foundry casting pit, and Tom had

Figure 6–6
Monument of the 20th Maine group

students rehearse the complex choreography necessary for a safe and successful pour. Once the metal was ready, a pair of students dressed in heat-resistant garments and protective headgear used long poles to hoist the glowing crucible from the furnace. As it rose, so too did the temperature in the room, even for observers standing dozens of feet away. Carrying it like a low-slung sedan chair to the casting pit, they prepared to pour; a third team member ladled off impurities at the top of the glowing crucible, which was lifted and tilted, pouring a stream of yellow-orange metal into the opening at the top of each mold (Figure 6–4). Throughout the hot, noisy process, Tom moved about, yelling out instructions, coaching, and making sure all movements were well coordinated. As the metal flowed, everything was on the line and our hearts were in our throats. It was scary to realize that some unseen weakspot in a mold might give way, destroying any chance for a successful pour and forcing that group to make an entirely new start on a prototype. In very different ways, Civil War soldiers and our students went through an ordeal by fire.

The foundry gods smiled, for all three pours went well. Students waited hours for the bronze to cool but returned at the earliest opportunity to break open the molds. Scraping and filing the tough shell material soon revealed the flawless forms of the monuments; having cast them in sections, the teams assembled them and applied protective patinas. Three infantrymen graced the monument of the 6th Wisconsin (Figure 6–5); on the side of its rectangular base were two narrative reliefs devoted to the regiment's heroic charge on the first day of the battle. The 69th Pennsylvania was celebrated with a giant minie ball (a rifle bullet with a conical head), perched on a square pedestal and capped by a color bearer with waving flag. Its powerful form signified that regiment's steadfastness in the face of Pickett's Charge. Finally, the 20th Maine group, saying that their regiment deserved a better monument than the one actually perched on Little Round Top, produced a round base carrying the image of their mustachioed commanding officer, Joshua Chamberlain (Figure 6–6).

While its monument moved toward completion, each group drafted and refined its writing projects. The most important of these was the text for the monument dedication speech. For inspiration, I distributed copies of half a dozen examples, written in the 1880s, to each group. We asked that the students give their literary efforts the same feeling of stylistic authenticity they had given their monuments. I believe this challenge made the project more engaging to those who normally found writing a drudge; in their attempts to capture the ring of a different era, many paid closer attention to matters of style than they ever had before. Reading student journals at the end of the course confirmed what our eyes and ears had already told us: all had done research on the history of their regiment, and all had helped design the artistic subject matter and inscriptions for the monuments. Similarly, all had contributed to the essential themes in their group's dedication speech and helped to edit the text.

In the eleventh week of the quarter, students gathered at my house, lugging their heavy monuments into the living room and depositing generous quantities of potluck food in the kitchen. With obvious pride and satisfaction, each group unveiled its monument: one member delivered the dedicatory oration and another reviewed its site plan. Words and objects, objects and words. . . . After generous applause and congratulations, we all sat down to a well-earned feast; the war was over and serenity reigned.

Conclusion

In offering an interdisciplinary course on Gettysburg and its monuments, our goal was never to supplant the experiences of reading and writing or the power of words with exercises in visual perception. Instead, Tom and I wanted to *integrate* meaningful exercises in visual and verbal modes of expression. Our teaching method was not a question of setting the verbal against the visual, but of allying the verbal and the visual, reinforcing both with empirical experience and challenges to the imagination. Expressed more concretely, we might ask who is more likely to learn something meaningful about the 20th Maine at Gettysburg: someone who reads an account of the battle and writes about it, someone who visits Little Round Top and sketches the site, someone who creates a sculpture of Joshua Chamberlain, or someone who does all three? I hope the answer is obvious.

This experience and that of similar courses I have taught have confirmed one of my intuitive feelings about education: well-designed exercises in reading and writing will make someone a far more perceptive interpreter of images, while the study of visual style will make someone a more perceptive reader and a better writer. This phenomenon, I believe, has broad implications for teaching in general, and not just for teachers of studio art or art history. Students in any discipline will understand something better if they don't simply hear about it but read and write about it too; moreover, visualizing it will almost certainly augment the learning process. Learners will understand an object or a space better if they describe it in words and sketch it as well as observe it. An effective way to study the relationship of ideas is not only to write about them, but to diagram them too. Human beings learn and create in a variety of ways; by engaging a broader range of our students' capacities and expressive modes, we as teachers, no matter what our discipline, can provide them with more meaningful and more effective learning experiences.

Response

PAMELA B. CHILDERS

D ick has hit on some key points in this chapter, and I like it for the following reasons:

- *The lessons learned in the monument design project go far beyond what we frequently do in a discipline-specific course.* As Dick states, "By combining the visual and the verbal, the course gave students multiple ways to internalize what they read and saw—and it enabled them to objectify what was so much a part of their own cultural history." Often we might encourage students to combine the visual and the verbal, but we allow them to get caught up in emotional reaction. We also need to emphasize the importance of *thinking* and *looking*, reading and writing.

- *The important role of collaboration in this project cannot be overlooked.* The backgrounds of Dick as historian and Tom as artist complement each other, as do their experience with writing across the curriculum. From the very start, the two instructors develop a cooperative involvement, make their goals and intentions clear to each other, and design a course that both are enthusiastic about teaching. Having been involved in such collaborations, I would emphasize how important their freewriting and sharing session is. It takes honesty and flexibility to make a collaboration work. Each instructor is also willing to take the time to make the course work effectively, with planning sessions, field trips, and so on.

- *Students are engaged and empowered throughout the course.* As Dick states, besides learning how the Civil War motivated memorial activities (verbal and visual), they want students to "experience the ability of both images and words to express powerful ideas and emotions [using monuments]." Although the teachers give the major assignments to enable students to have a common foundation of knowledge and experience, they also encourage students to take over the classes by leading discussions, selecting what group they will represent in the major project, and creating their own original models. In other words, the teachers become the facilitators once the students have mastered what they need to know.

- *The hands-on experience helps students overcome their fear of taking risks.* The students who are not artists fear testing their visual skills or exposing them to the scrutiny of "real artists"; those who are studio art majors fear showing their verbal weaknesses. Dick describes this problem as "but a single manifestation of a dichotomy endemic in the western cultural tradition: *the visual and physical are often set in opposition and subjugated to the verbal and intellectual."* With teachers like Dick and Tom, these students are inspired to get involved visually, verbally, *and* intellectually through the use of tangible objects, such as the historical artifacts loaned by a local historian.

- *This course is a true multimedia experience for students and teachers.* To the visual Dick and Tom add aural and tactile devices to immerse students in their learning and elicit a verbal response. From the opening day of class when they play Dvořák's *American Quartet* and show slides of Gettysburg and its monuments, these teachers include as many of the senses as possible. Handling Civil War guns in a classroom or walking the ground and examining statues at Gettysburg provide learning experiences that reading and class lectures cannot offer.

- *Finally, Dick and Tom make clear the connection between the visual and the verbal.* The course projects involve teams modeled after those that designed monuments in the late nineteenth century. Yes, the teachers select the teams, but their selection is based on surveys intended to balance talent, just as similar committees would have done in the previous century. As involved as students are in the connection of all these elements, the teachers have kept their criteria credible historically and create a *real* visual and writing project.

Thematic Variations

Assumptions

Before I talk about variations on this assignment, I want to make several points. It is perhaps wise to remember that most secondary teachers do not have the luxury of such a small class, an entire quarter to devote to one topic, the financial means or facilities to cast monuments in bronze, or the flexability to take class trips out of town. For many, just planning a one-hour bus trip to and from a site becomes a jungle of paperwork, permission slips, chaperones, class coverage, funds, and so on. Now that we have established these assumptions, let's look at some ways we can apply what Dick has so beautifully described.

Involving Students Visually and Verbally

Since this chapter has established that images and words can express powerful ideas and emotions, let's try a few possibilities. Several years ago, I worked with my students on writing persuasive essays and satire. Some just didn't seem to get the point. A cousin of one of the students, a political cartoonist, visited our class and explained that images in his cartoons conveyed strong emotions but in a different way than their essays. The ability to draw an idea that would take several pages to explain in words impressed students. But they said such things as, "You're talented," "You don't understand what we're trying to say." To make his point, the artist asked them to take a strong stand on an issue of importance to them; together they created a political cartoon. The cartoon shows the performers taking all the gold medals, posing, smiling, and pushing the writers out of the spotlight. The students saw their feeling that performers get the glory for "performing" what the writers have created and clearly presented it in the cartoon. Whenever students have difficulty getting started on a persuasive essay, I have them look at the cartoon to remember how we visualize what we feel.

Perhaps a collection of political cartoons demonstrating a particular point of view in a history class, or any course, could begin the process of writing. Students could draw their own cartoons to express their point of view on the issue and refer to their cartoons to focus on the factors they want to mention in an essay.

Civil War Trip Variations

The trip to the Gettysburg battlefield is an extravagance for many of us, but the idea could work just as well in any town with a war memorial or public statue. An activity for a history class, an American literature class, or an art class might be to research the town or city, find out the building restrictions for a memorial or statue, and examine existing physical spaces and historical sites in the immediate area. Teams of students would research and design a memorial for the town, find an appropriate site, meet town requirements, and write the inscription and a dedication speech. Some communities might even encourage such a project and build the best design. A national bricklayers' association in one city held a contest to elicit designs for works of art for a restored section of town. The bricklayers built the winning designs and the designers received a cash award and participated in the construction.

Connecting the Visual and Verbal with Hands-On Activities

While watching a television news show one evening, I learned about a successful photographer who has given up his career to teach students in an inner city school how to use cameras. By having students focus on others, the photographer has taught them how to see, to question, and to critique. A series of the photographs, accompanied by a statement from the student photographers about the composition and subject are now on display at the city art museum. This is a powerful way to teach writing: by encouraging students to focus on something, photograph it, develop the film, and write about the photograph. The result is a composition that is visual and verbal.

Michael Lowry, a biology teacher, uses a hands-on activity along with writing as his 45-minute unit test. Students have access to clay, colored pens and pencils, scissors, and colored paper. In this limited time, they are asked to demonstrate their knowledge of cells by using any of these materials to create a model of, for example, a phase of mitosis. As each student completes his or her model, Michael photographs it and gives the Polaroid print to the student, who moves on to the writing center to write a description of it. The photograph is stapled to the finished text and submitted to the teacher before the end of the period. It is amazing how fast students are able to complete the process.

Michael and I have spoken about using a video camera or digital camera the next time so the pictures are larger and clearer, but that would eliminate the immediacy of having the picture nearby during writing—students often put their photos in the paper stand and look at them as they type. A student's knowledge of a particular concept, applied in a visual world with hands-on involvement and expressed in writing, becomes a tool for learning in new ways.

Constructing Narratives

Dick and Tom's narrative history word game may sound aural and verbal, but it also involves spatial skill. I see some other possibilities. When I teach Whitman's "Song of Myself" in American literature courses, I have students pick their favorite lines to bring to class. Then we go around the room reading our first choices, even if someone else has already read those lines. Students begin to see the importance of repetition and pattern in a poem. We then read the same lines going around the room in the other direction and vote on which order is more effective. Rhythm, rhyme, balance of ideas, connection of images all become part of our discussion. What if students also brought in a visual image with the lines they selected? We could try them in different sequences to see how the images work with the written words. I want to try this a few times to see if the visual reinforces the structure of the poem. I think my next natural inclination would be to ask students to pick a visual that is not theirs and try to respond to it in a fresh twentieth-century Whitmanesque line.

Again, in classes across the disciplines, I can think of ways that teachers could encourage a better understanding of the construction of narratives by using visuals. For schools with performing arts programs, such collaborative activities are natural. Dance, television, drama, music, and writing majors can form teams to create their own civilizations once they have been given some background on civilizations that have existed and survived. We did such an activity at Red Bank Regional, grouping students so that there were representatives of each major on every team. Each team had to create a language and a culture with its own set of myths or religion. The teams were given a week, meeting one period per day, before the presentations began. In their evaluations of this project, students mentioned how much they missed a written language and found that to be an important step after they began to create visual interpretations of what they were trying to say. Body language, sounds, and visual interpretation became extremely important. They certainly appreciated their own language after this exercise.

If any man has any poetry in him he should paint it, for it has
all been said and written, and they have hardly begun to paint
it. Every man who has that gift should paint.
—Dante Gabriel Rossetti

Beyond Visualizing a Community of Learners

Joan A. Mullin

Although our culture comprises both visual and verbal images, students know that school culture for the most part promotes the latter. When the visual is brought into the classroom, it is more often for relief from the day-to-day (a movie) and the ordinary (a TV show), or as a stimulus for writing a paper. These are valuable when they're part of a larger instructional plan (often they are not), but they still fragment and separate the visual from the verbal: seeing (the visual) from writing (the verbal). Even when visual images are used in the classroom, their component parts—organization, color, image, placement, and so on—involve separate acts of seeing and writing and thus never tap into the intimate bond between image and language. Moreover, these activities do not take advantage of the place where critical thinking may actuate itself: by working at the intersection of the visual and verbal, students can draw upon images that make visible their conception of an idea, and teachers can see whether students have understood or whether they are merely repeating information.

Creating opportunities for students to work at the intersection of language and vision supports what we know about language in theory and through practical experience. Recent neurobiological research by Mark Sereno at the University of California at San Diego provides another promising link. Sereno's primary area of research is the neurological architecture of vision in primates and rodents, and he has developed a complex interdisciplinary theory about brain evolution and the origins of human language.

Reduced to almost haiku proportions, Sereno's idea is this: language ability arose in the human brain not through the development of a new, uniquely human language organ, as most accounts have it, but by "a relatively minor rewiring" of a neural system. That was already there. And that neural wiring belonged largely to the visual system, a part of the brain that recent research—including Sereno's own—has shown to be almost unimaginably complex. (Gutin 1996, 84)

It would seem advantageous to stimulate the visual connection when we want to improve verbal articulation.

The Problem: Theirs, Mine, and Ours

Introducing activities that ask students to produce a concrete visual representation arouses all the anxieties experienced in childhood. Despite what art educators know about the importance of encouraging original expression in children, few of us grow up without a sense of artistic inadequacy. By the second grade, most of us know who is a "good drawer" and who is not; by middle school, familiar names appear and reappear on the walls of the art room; in any high school everyone knows who can produce graphics for the newspaper or artwork for the group project. Moreover, since so few students seem capable of producing "art" (something good enough to be sold for profit), many schools ignore or marginalize these activities. Art is also one of the first program budgets to be cut when fiscal prudence deems it necessary. Thus, convincing adolescent and adult students to engage in visual activities means changing their minds about the role of the visual in cognitive development.

As I do with any classroom method that will encounter student reluctance, I first talk with the class about why I am asking them to do something—in this case, I discuss the connection between the visual and verbal. Students quickly point to the visual impact of advertising (billboards, commercials, magazine ads), music videos, CD covers, and book jackets. Thanks to TV, movies, talk shows, and pop psychology, students already believe that what one produces by hand often reflects the inner workings of the mind. So it is not difficult to convince them that their own artistic creations might well reveal a key to how they think about a subject they are studying. Students are eager to discover further insights into themselves. The first time I connected the activity described below to the course material being studied, we were all amazed at the results. In successive iterations of the activity in writing classes at the high school and college levels, I continue to be pleasantly surprised at how revelatory and engaging it continues to be.

The idea started forming a few years ago when a poet-colleague at the university and I taught an experimental upper-level writing-intensive class on visual language. We hoped that by focusing students' attention on their own visual experiences, they would experience the collaborative nature of interpretation, sharpen their observational skills, and explore the intersections of the visual and the verbal. The course would include slides, videos, guided museum trips, students' drawings and journal writing, readings and discussions of artwork (e.g., by Paul Klee's *On Modern Art*), and use of the famous Bareiss book collection of rare books, many by artists, at the Toledo Museum of Art.

Since my colleague was the primary instructor, and I was there in the capacity of writing consultant, I had the luxury of observing how the students interacted and how they reacted to the works presented. We tried many writing activities and tried to set up collaborative groups to work on responses to material, but students primarily sought out my colleague (who was the official grader) for direction, worked alone, and failed miserably at collaborating. As I watched students wrestle with the concept of visual language, a major problem stood out: Although we looked at many visual images, most students kept trying to define the "language" of these images in words. And there was another problem: I didn't know the students' names.

Drawing on my earlier experiences with the visual (Mullin 1994) and a previous experiment in a composition class, I designed an activity that

- identified and named a community of learners
- provided practice in effective feedback and critique
- established a vocabulary for articulating visual concepts

I have since discovered that this activity can be tailored to classes in other subject areas to identify the visual characteristics of a subject area (especially abstract areas) and to create a collaborative working identity among students at all levels.

Creating a Solution

I wanted to get to know the students in the course, but I also wanted to know how each of them was beginning to define visual language. Most of class discussion had been tentative, and many students were reluctant to articulate a personal definition. This might be because images defy our descriptions, and lacking a vocabulary, we often lapse into cliché.

The other problem—students' identity—seemed to be related to the lack of participation and collaboration in class. It is always easier for me to remember students' names when I associate them with their ideas: individuals assume a personality. But students were reluctant to participate and hesitant as most basic writers are to share their thoughts when they had little encouragement, practice, or success. It seemed ironic that so many students could not express themselves in a class exploring how meaning was carried through signs, how groups or individuals create signs to carry meaning, and how a group comes to agree on or explore the interpretation of those signs. I was aware of only the few voices that dominated discussions.

One day I arranged on a side table an assortment of tools and visually interesting materials: colored paper, lick and stick strips in fluorescent shades, pieces of patterned wrapping paper, glitter, stars, ribbons, colored foam, packing materials, corks, buttons, colored pencils, crayons, markers, chalk, tacks, scissors, glue (colored and white), tape, staples, and paper clips. As students wandered in, their eyes went to the table. "Is this for us?" they asked. "What do we get to do?" I told them yes, but they would have to wait and wondered whether another element had been lacking: the tactile and textural experience offered through the visual.

I told the students something along these lines: I had trouble remembering their names. We were studying visual language. I wanted them to create a tag that would represent their definition of visual language and serve as a name tag. I wanted to know who they were conceptually in this class. Since I made it clear that this name tag was to be their own creation, there were none of the usual questions about "how long," "how big," or what form the tag should take. They could use any of the materials on the table, should share tools but work alone, keeping their eyes on their own work. They would have twenty minutes or so for this task. When they were done, they were to place their tags in a cardboard box in the center of the room and go about cleaning up their own area. When I said they could start, they rushed for their materials and got to work.

Prior to this project, the class had been typical of many: all of us could count on a few students to participate, most students were willing to sit back and be talked to, interaction was limited to those students with whom they sat or whom they already knew. The class was held in a studiolike room, where we sat around an open rectangle of tables, and eye contact had been limited to the instructor or the text in front of each person. That day, the atmosphere in the classroom changed dramatically: there were calls for scissors, giggles, friendly jostling for materials, polite requests for the "blue star paper when you are through," queries about "Who has the black marker?"

I gave them a ten-minute, and then a five-minute warning as I also completed my tag. Oddly enough, everyone finished within the time allotted, most within the last five minutes.

When all the tags were in the box, all the mess righted, and all the students seated, I took the box and walked around the room asking each person to take one tag, not his or her own, and study it. I asked them to think about what this object represented—what it said, how it said it—and to explain why they read that meaning into it. Since this was to denote a name, I asked them to think about

- what this object said to them about that person's definition of visual language
- how the object named the person and the concept

I said they should study their piece and whoever wanted to should begin. Patience paid off; as the silence got heavier, someone shrugged and said, "I guess I'll start."

Students talked about the tag they held, and when they finished, I would ask whose work it was. Once the creator was identified, the person who described the name tag would carry it over to the owner and present it. This ritual provided the necessary break between each description. The class progressed, sometimes with moments of silence between presentations, sometimes with two people starting at the same time and then negotiating who would speak. Once everyone finished, I asked for observations from the class on two levels:

1. What definitions of visual language emerged?
2. What did they notice about the class itself during this activity?

The Results: Part One

From the beginning I had clearly stated that a definition of visual language would emerge from this class. But afterwards, students commented that they now realized there were contending definitions, and that some of those definitions were dependent upon disciplinary perspectives. Rather than privileging anyone's answer, students began to collect possible answers. This approach opened up the possibilities and freed students from looking for a correct (teacher-provided) definition. And since the tag was intended to represent themselves and their own names, students knew that each one would be different, that while one's talent was important, it was not significant. As one student pointed out: "I have no artistic talent, but then, that's part of who I am—a nonartist. So, I didn't care if this didn't look like a van Gogh." I would not claim that competition was never a factor, but each time I have tried this exercise, students become totally involved in producing a personal piece, one that signifies them alone. The individuality is reflected in the analytical responses.

When a nineteen-year-old female student picked up the name tag shown in Figure 7–1, she responded:

> This person's life is filled with a variety of activities. She—I think it's a she—feels very positive about all the variety in her life: as if it was a gift. I think that's why these ribbons stream out from the horn; life for her is an endless package she opens—'cause, look, as you go deeper into the horn, there's all kinds of little icons stuffed in there: one is a kid, one looks like a pair of shoes, dance shoes, so she must be a dancer. There are crayons and paper represented, so she must have something to do with art or maybe teaching kids. Everything in here is some aspect of her life. The colors are all bright and this gives me a positive, busy, energetic feeling.
>
> I think for her, visual language would be connected to art—that it's something you, you know, do. I mean, look at this! It's the biggest name tag here, and so elaborate! This person likes color, action; it's all out there.

When Patty received the cornucopia she had made, she agreed that the analysis was pretty close: she was a dancer and taught dance as well as art in a local school system. As a mother, she was busy all the time, loved what she did, and continued to feel blessed by all that was given her. Whether in her church, at home, or in school, she confessed, she worked art into the lives around her through lessons and activities, or by offering to put up bulletin boards or help with set designs.

The forty-something, poet-instructor carefully described another tag:

> This person likes color. It's a simple card, really, with all the colors of the rainbow in stripes across one side of this 3 × 5 card. Regular rows, drawn straight, but freehand, and colored in with pencil. I'd say this is a woman who is into rainbows and color. But on the other side there's this; here, you probably can't see it. There's just a small rectangle in the middle of the back of the card, drawn in regular lead pencil, with the word "me" inside. She seems to be talking about two sides of herself: maybe this is the public one, the contained person, and this is the one inside or vice versa. Maybe she's colorful outside and very closed in and small inside. Maybe it's both. On the other hand, you know, this could be a young man coming to grips with the female side of his personality. You know, he's trying to find out how all of this—these two sides—fit together.

Figure 7–1
Patty's name tag

When Ray, a young man, received his name tag, he grinned sheep-ishly and said that was about right. Always quiet before, Ray agreed that there were two sides of him that he was exploring. Although he didn't respond much more than that during the class, he later made a point of telling me how important the activity and analysis were to him: he was exploring his sexuality and deciding to come out. The rainbow he drew referred to the one used by gay rights activists.

Holding the tag shown in Figure 7–2, a traditional college student (woman) reacted:

> This has got to be a woman! Okay, she took strips of pink paper and made this incredible sphere—like a biosphere! On the inside of the sphere is trapped, no caught, no I guess she is placed inside. I think she's just feeling fragile, delicate, I mean this whole piece, you feel like you have to be very careful holding it. I think she sees herself that way, maybe as protected by her pink world.

Sandy quietly chuckled when she received her name tag. She pointed out that what had been overlooked was her name on the inside; that the pink, of course, stands for all the "girl" stuff. She pointed out that while we had been spending a lot of time in class talking about artists' renditions of language and the word, we had not yet looked at

Figure 7–2
Sandy's name tag

what any women artists said. So, Sandy insisted, her womblike name tag was also a response to the lack of representation of women in the class (a situation that was remedied by the next class meeting).

The Results: Part Two

The original goals of this activity were to help me visually associate names with persons and to see what kinds of conceptual representations of visual language students could produce. We met these goals but went much further:

- I was able to remember students' names because I had a conceptual and visual association for each one of them.
- I asked students to wear their tags or place them in front of them for the next class, and about half of them brought in their tags and pinned them on or placed them on the table in front of them for the next couple of weeks.
- Students began talking to each other before and after class, calling each other by name, and interacting during class discussion (this also occurred during a similar experience in another class).
- This new community extended beyond that quarter's course. According to students I see on campus (and those who have left but still e-mail me), they still remember each other from that class, or, as one student said, "When I see people from that class, I say hi to them on campus—I don't do that usually because I don't really get to know others in my classes."

This sense of connection was heightened by the ritual action of delivering each name tag to its owner—by knowing that one would have to get up, walk around the room, and hand the tag to whoever created it. When we discussed the activity afterwards, students pointed out how aware they were that they were holding someone else's work—that this object was an expression of who that person was. As a result (and this is something we all observed) they handled each piece carefully, as if they were handling the person. Indeed, that was an apt analogy, for in this case each person's idea was concretely visible, and each person's conceptual self was equally vulnerable to critique. Here and in other classes, the project engendered respect for ideas and a genuine willingness to listen to each other. Students commented that they were careful about how they said anything because they wanted others to be as careful with their name tag. Some indicated that the activity provided them with an opportunity to see what others thought. Student evaluations suggested that the exercise had made them think about visual literacy through personal engagement. One student commented that he felt the pressure wasn't on him to answer a question; we were building an idea together, so he felt "safe to participate" in that attempt. Finally, the activity produced a vocabulary from which we could continue to look at other works.

Of course, at the conclusion of the activity, we also discussed what these pieces said about visual language—a topic we had not always addressed during the name tag analysis. Students later said they were more interested in the personal revelation within the visual representation. If they were so drawn to the personal, I asked, was visual representation and interpretation in general largely personal? This discussion resulted in a number of class-generated questions that could well have served as a guideline for the rest of the quarter:

- If visual representation is personal, are there universal human elements to it?
- What do colors mean in other cultures and how did they come to take on those meanings?
- If colors have meaning in other cultures, what about shapes? objects? placement?
- What does gender have to do with how one uses visuals? language?
- Does a viewer read gender? How does one learn to do that?
- How did we learn what visuals stood for?
- What is the role of parents? school? media? in shaping what we think of visuals?
- Has media extended our ability to represent the world, or does it homogenize the way we are supposed to see the world? And who dictates what we're supposed to see?
- If we are supposed to become visually literate, what language do we then learn?
- Is it necessary to analyze a visual representation in order to enjoy and understand it?
- Is it appropriate to use language to describe a three-dimensional representation?

As these questions shaped our areas of inquiry, we all began to look at how others wrestled with them, adding to our shared vocabulary. We uncovered far more questions than answers, the high quality of students' final art/written projects represented their deep engagement with these questions. Among other items, we received

- a small felt bag of handmade tiles etched with an imaginary alphabet one could almost understand
- a research paper illuminated like a medieval manuscript
- a fully developed cartoon strip
- a series of prints exploring shades, light, and the alphabet
- a uniquely personal alphabet book for a child of handmade paper sewn together

The name tag activity encouraged lively discussions and achieved a heightened awareness of the role of critique and response. When students pointed out the care with which they handled each other's work, they also discovered that evaluating anything, including written texts, is a personal engagement between the maker and the audience. On their own they began to talk about

- point of view
- the importance of asking questions about a work
- producing not judgments but responses, for which there must be reasons

Students also discovered that some of their reasons for responding to a work in certain ways might well be based on a very personal experience, an aversion, an assumption. They began to discuss their own vulnerability in being evaluated, agreeing that at least within this class, we saw assessment as a part of learning. Students believed that since we were all struggling, feedback from each other contributed to our growing understanding. I always encourage the discussion in this direction, but students noted that the atmosphere in class that particular day was very different, very caring and communal. It wasn't difficult to drop the inner critic each of us carry. The "competitive jousting" that usually exists in our classrooms had no place that day.

Summary and Repercussions

In that class I learned the names of students, but what is more important is that they had also taken on identities for each other. We were more comfortable as a class. Discussion involved many more students, and the initial excitement about this new class was furthered by their own inquiry. Perhaps one of the best results was that this newly bonded community of learners did not end at the door of the classroom. I still communicate with students from this class, which took place three years ago, and I asked two of them, via e-mail, what they remembered about the name tag activity.

Sandy (of the pink womblike sphere) replied:

You know, I remember that day in class in a sort of surreally vivid way, I'm not sure if it's because I had just read *Mrs. Dalloway* and everything looked that way, or if the name tags gave me a heightened awareness of myself, but I remember wearing a long blue and orange batik print dress with my black sweater tied around my waist. I took the bus to the art museum [where we had class], and I sat between Charlie and Ray. Making the name tags I was thinking about Christmas tree ornaments my family has, ugly ones. They're shaped like eggs and you have to sort of look inside the egg and there's a little crèche or something. I wanted you to have to look inside and change perspectives a little to see my name, come into my own territory. And I wanted pink, pink for girls, it was something I needed to do in order to get my bearings at the time. When we traded name tags and heard ours interpreted by someone else, I was thinking "Okay, yeah, could be" as someone described me as fragile and delicate, careful about coming out of my shell. I was surprised to see you shaking your head thinking she had it wrong. Later, when we talked about it, you told me I might want to "revise my self-image" if I understood myself as fragile and delicate. So that had me thinking all day.

Charlie had been writing a cartoon strip for his tag . . . he wanted to work for Disney when he was done with school. I wonder where he is? And of course I remember the person who read a random group of squiggles as Charlie. Knowing that it belonged to neither Charlie [in the class], I was interested in how language appears where none is intended. I was thinking that literary criticism does the same and shouldn't. Someone made a simple rainbow the size of a 3 × 5 index card I remember, and we were so caught up in gender after my project that whoever was guessing decided it had to be a female person, and of course, it was a man. Ken's was in rainbow colors too, wasn't it? And it looked like a cross between a paint brush and a wrench. I was surprised by how few people incorporated their written name into theirs. Maybe they hadn't time, but I honestly think it didn't occur to people; the project had taken on a nonliteral dimension.

Ray, another student, remembered:

Oh, name tags. Mine was pretty forgettable. It was a series of labels: white, male, college student, something like that, with "More Than This" on the last card you turned. I was going through my white male anxiety phase at that time. Plus, suffering from lack of creativity. Myself, I loved the stuff other folks did with tags, and the interpretation part was very interesting, mainly because it showed the discrepancy between what you thought you'd put out there, and what others thought you were displaying. I remember Jack's vividly, that thing with wild colors. He was neat. Is he still there? I

remember he'd just come back after a long absence, had been in the
Navy, and was interested in archetypes.

My name tag experience was pretty good, subdued, not flashy,
like me, and yet it talked a lot, so it was somewhat accurate, more in
retrospect than at the time.

In these and other conversations, students from the course remembered people and details but also continued to reflect on the impact of visual interpretation, of language. What we discovered as a
class about visual language (as well as about visuals and language)
was best summed up in Ray's final words: "You reveal yourself more
in your pretensions and attempts to put something solid of yourself
out there than you often know. I mean, other things besides what you
think you are putting out there."

Implications for Other Classrooms

The first class in which I used this approach was a college composition
class, and I used it primarily to learn students' names. I didn't connect
it to the course objectives (though I should have done so). At first I
thought this visual language class project was so successful only because visual language was our content. But then I began to explore
other possibilities. I taught an Honors Readings Conference course,
basically a traditional great books course, with an expanded canon,
which covered literature from the twelfth to the beginning of the
eighteenth century. After a few introductory discussions and readings,
I asked the class to create name tags that represented their concept of
this time period. Since the texts included, among others, Abelard and
Heloise's letters, Dante's *Inferno*, *The Confessions of Lady Nijo*, and Mon-
taigne's *Essays*, students had a range of perspectives they could draw
on and draw together. Of all the shapes and convolutions students
created, what impressed all of us was the array of color—or lack of it.
Why would some associate this period with brilliant color and others
with darkness? This led to questions about illuminated texts, our assumptions about the Dark Ages, the place and evolution of art during
this period, the place of metaphor in the art of logic—and we had
plenty of examples. We also ended up with a lot of questions to research and invited campus experts to come in and help us understand
some of the questions—and misconceptions—we had generated.

Another significant result: the class bonded. While this may
sound irrelevant, those who teach honors students in large competitive settings know that, too often, students are in such intense competition with each other that they focus on performing in class rather
than contributing to the community of learners, or they focus on

manufacturing a product rather than challenging themselves to take inquiry risks. As a result, while honors classes may appear to be ideal—several students participate and most complete high quality work—students are often involved in the game of giving the teacher what he or she wants, of doing only enough work to get the A they need, of reducing learning to formula. What is often missing is a community of learners contributing to each other's knowledge-making, students willing to take risks by following challenging questions or by writing about subjects that cannot be tied up in formulaic papers.

In one of the honors classes, we began talking about how important names are in our culture, how the sound of a name produces images. This led to a discussion of language and expression, and somehow, to an argument over papers and five-paragraph themes. Caught using my own jargon ("five-paragraph-theme"), I was asked what is wrong with this kind of writing. What began as a discussion of names ended in a heated discussion of writing theory, with the students challenging some of my own assumptions about how and why they write according to formula. The discussion also provided students with a forum for asking questions about writing they had never asked before. We decided that we were being too abstract, that we needed concrete evidence before we continued the discussion, so we agreed to write two papers on the same topic—one in five-paragraph form and one that ended without a pat answer, that explored rather than gave definitive answers. We composed these together and then discussed the visual and verbal differences. The results are worth another chapter, but the point here is that this level of interaction and learning grew out of the name tag activity.

The activity does not work only in college classes or with honors students. I asked a colleague who teaches high school in a multicultural urban setting if I could use this activity in her class of juniors and seniors. I had intended to have them relate their name tag making to American literature, but when I got to the class I learned that all week they had been writing letters of application to college or for summer jobs. What I then asked them to do was to represent in visual form who they were, what they thought made them unique enough to be chosen by this college or that employer. With the same enthusiasm as their college counterparts, these high school students went to work. They were noisier and they teased each other because they were friends, but their diligence and concentration were equal to any college or honors class. What is more, their analyses were just as insightful, their name tags as varied, creative, and individual, and the activity itself as useful for class discussions in the following weeks. When asked to evaluate the activity (anonymously), students responded:

It was a little scary to see what I had done and what [Elissa] said about me. She could read me like a book just from what I did, and she was right!

At first I thought this was just a stupid thing to do, but then I started thinking about who I was and what I was saying in my college letters! It was boring what I wrote! I'm more interesting than that! I'm going back and rewrite my letters.

When I walked thru the hall with my name, everybody looked at it and I was proud. I started thinking about what else I could of done. Who else was I?

I took my name tag home and put it on the refrigerator. There it sits, a constant reminder of who I am and what I have accomplished.

It sits on my dresser now and I feel like it's a little piece of me there that I can look at and think about. I pick it up and turn it around thinking about how this might look in three years, or five years.

These responses can serve as a resource for other ways of using this activity across age levels and disciplines:

- Have students make name tags as an ice breaker activity at the beginning of the year or semester; repeat the activity at the end of the year and accompany with a compare-and-contrast paper. Students often don't have a sense of how far they have come in a term or what they have learned. This is one way of concretely demonstrating their own learning.

- Instead of having an oral analysis of the name tags, use them as a writing experience to launch into a discussion of symbol, color, point of view.

- Include the name tags in student portfolios. If students create one at the beginning and end of the year, have them speak to their progress as writers, visualizers, and thinkers. If portfolios travel with students from year to year, the tags can serve as a stimulus for self, peer, or teacher assessment.

- Use name tags as resources for writing a character sketch or story.

- Ask students to create a name tag that exemplifies how they perceive individuals in a particular cultural or historical context (if you were a Puritan, what would your name tag be? If you lived during the 1960s, etc.). Students then take on an identity that reveals misconceptions, prior knowledge, and assumptions about that period.

Name tags function as visible windows to students' ideas, not as activities that "break up the day" or "give the kids (and you) a breather." The application of this activity across disciplines is limited only by imagination and your willingness as a teacher to allow students to use their visual faculties, which precede conceptual language, to explore how they are processing images or concepts, what they already know, or what they have learned.

It seems foolish to ignore not only the practices of many teaching professionals who find visual pedagogy a powerful teaching tool, but also the mounting scientific evidence that supports this pedagogy. While the technical equipment to prove Sereno's biological theories is only now being developed, he has drawn on his extensive interdisciplinary studies—in linguistics, communication systems of animals, philosophy, and the neurological architecture of vision (Gutin 1996, 83)—to pose a persuasive theory that traditional language theorists must now disprove. Over twenty-five years ago he "began to see a similarity between what the mysterious language system in the brain was doing as it tacked together the meaning extracted from individual words in a series, and what the visual system was doing as it put together the information gathered from a series of glances. If the mental tasks were so similar [he wondered], why couldn't the brain be using some of the same wiring?" (86).

As Sereno and his colleagues discover more about the connections between visual processing and language ability, the demand for pedagogy that supports, enriches, and enhances the interconnective system will grow. But teachers and students can begin now to create the community and the means by which we will name those concepts in startlingly new visual and verbal ways.

Response

ERIC H. HOBSON

I like the name tag activity Joan describes because

- *It is simple.* You don't need a great variety of materials to pull it off: construction paper, card stock, even plain white copy paper works with whatever motley mix of writing/coloring tools happen to be hanging around on office desks or in the recesses of desk drawers, or can be borrowed from children's crayon and marker stashes.

- *It is novel.* Students, particularly those in high school and college, maintain well-rehearsed "cool poses" about learning and the extent to which they should participate willingly and enthusiastically. Their expectations about what happens in English classes, for example, come up short when they enter the classroom and find the enticing clutter of paper, crayons, and scissors Joan described. Preconceptions and pretensions fade away, and what often emerges, even among adult learners, is that part of the students' personalities that enjoys fun and a challenge. The payoff is powerful: attention to task and a predisposition to learn because their defenses are lowered.

- *It is flexible.* As described, the name tag activity can be used with students from all levels and for a number of purposes. It is also an activity, however, that can be modified in a great number of ways. This flexibility contributes to its potential for a long shelf life. Classroom activities that successfully infiltrate teachers' lesson plans are those that offer more than one use for more than one situation.

Thematic Variation

Since Joan first introduced me to the name tag project, I have tried it out on several occasions in a variety of writing courses. In each early instance, however, I used it as a stopgap measure, more to fill in the schedule than to serve as an integral part of the writing course. The following comments detail a more recent use of the activity in which it served to provide both the initial activity for a writing course and the medium by which I was able to establish the course's goals in terms of what concept I expected the students to deal with and learn to apply to their writing.

The Situation

I recently taught an advanced composition course in a highly compact and intense format (three ten-hour weekend sessions: three hours Friday night; seven hours Saturday) to a group of adult students working toward special education certification. The students were enrolled in an extension program designed to train special educators for rural and poor school districts that cannot, due to these communities' low pay scales and isolation, attract special educators from outside the immediate area. Given the course's truncated nature, my goal for the course was straightforward, even minimal, compared to the traditional semester-long version of the course: to change how they thought about themselves as writers. I wanted to work as much on the metacognitive level as on the level of text production. The most reasonable goal to strive for in three weekends was to get these students to think about

- how they think about writing
- how those thoughts influence (positively and negatively) their ability to write at the level demanded by their college curriculum and the professional community they are working to join

To start the discussion, and their transformation, I decided we would need to discuss how to analyze an audience and why thinking carefully about who would read their writing is important to their success as writers (and often liberating, making writing an easier task than it might have been in their past experience).

The Group

The thirty students ranged in age from early twenties to late fifties, and most were in the program as part of the retraining they required in order to begin second careers. Several of the men had worked most of their adult lives in the local coal strip mines, which had closed as tightening environmental laws reduced demand for the local, highly sulfurous coal. Many of the women were displaced from jobs in the garment industry, which had moved offshore in search of cheaper labor. At least six of the women were long-term housewives forced into the labor pool by a husband's disabilitating injury and illness or as a result of divorce.

Their college-level educational experiences were mixed. Some had junior college credit; two men had attended college for a year or two; one had a B.S. degree in journalism; for most their formal education had stopped at high school graduation.

With one exception, these students did not have much experience with writing, nor did they view writing as something they did well or had much hope of improving. The class consensus was, for the most part, "let's suffer through these three weekends together and just get it over with." During discussions in and out of the class, it was clear that writing, other than letters to family members and friends, played a negligible role in their day-to-day lives. What writing they recalled doing was linked almost exclusively to schoolwork and was viewed as a chore to complete.

The Problem

Because I am a visual learner and very poor at remembering the names of people I have only just met, Joan's name tag activity offered me hope. I took a chance and greeted the students on the first night with a supply-covered table. The second, more important reason for choosing this activity with these students was strategic: if I could just get these not-too-confident writers to think carefully about issues of audience, they would accomplish something of educational value in an otherwise troublesome setting. I knew that lecturing to them about audience would hurt my chances of getting through at the very start of the course. These students came to the first session having put in full days and a full week at work, many without going home or eating dinner before driving in. A lecture would encourage their passivity as well as reinforcing their bias that writing classes (English, to them) are inherently boring and tedious. Making name tags was active, and even if I had to spend twenty to thirty minutes of the first session cutting and gluing paper and other materials with the students, it would be time well spent.

Tasks

Stage One: Collect and Distribute Names Tags. Like Joan, I collected the finished name tags after about thirty minutes, placing them in a box to hide them from view. Following a fifteen-minute "introduction to the course" session, I circulated around the room asking each student to reach into the box and draw out a name tag (if they picked their own, they returned it to the box quickly and chose another).

Stage Two: Observe (5 minutes). With name tag in front of them, the students were to look at the tag and nothing else for five minutes

(I had to reassure them several times that I was serious.). During that time they were to notice as much as they could about the tag's features and construction.

Stage Three: Record Details (3 minutes). With only three minutes to complete the task, students were to record or list as many of their observations about the name tag as possible.

Stage Four: Draw Inferences about Author (10 minutes). While they were recording details, I wrote the following instructions on the board and gave them ten minutes to complete their responses:

> Without trying to guess who it is, describe the person who made the name tag in front of you. What does it tell you about them? How does it get this message across?

Amid groans and protests, the students began, and with an occasional note of encouragement along the lines of "Keep going, keep pushing the description," and "You still have several minutes to use," students wrote descriptions that were notable for a number of reasons. Most wrote multiparagraphed texts of several hundred words (many admitted they would not have believed they could have written that much on any topic). Most responded in great detail, although employing a variety of formats (such as narratives, lists, objective/third-person observations). Most responded without getting too worried about whether they were writing well or correctly (again the majority admitted that previously they almost always worried about these issues).

Stage Five: Develop a Strategy for Working with this Person (10 minutes). I added a further instruction:

> You have just been informed that the person who made the name tag you hold will be your partner in a very important project. Take ten minutes and develop a plan for establishing the best working relationship possible using the information you have gathered so far. What should you remember to do/not do and say/not say.

Stage Six: Presentating Name Tag Authors (3–5 minutes per student). Students presented their conclusions about their name tag creator and the strategy they would use to work productively with this person on a project. Although the first two or three speakers were somewhat hesitant, soon the class was so involved in their descriptions and strategies, I had to call time for every subsequent presenter in order to move the process along. Also, although I had not said that the makers should identify themselves, after someone gasped at how accurately the recipient of her name tag had read her, we all identified ourselves after our tag was discussed. And, more often than not, the readings were accurate and revealing.

The Outcome

Although I had yet to talk specifically about the writing process or specific assignments for the course, students had participated in what amounted to an intensive two-hour workshop exploring audience and effective strategies. We had covered much of the same ground I would have covered in a lecture but in a manner that fit the show-me-how-it-works learning style typical of these students.

During the final hour, we discussed audience and how to adapt one's writing to meet a reader's needs. We chose three particularly interesting name tags and placed them at the head of the conference table, established our task as one of writing an informational report to explain to these three people what abilities a special education curriculum should develop in prospective special educators, and raised the following questions:

- What questions about special education might these people ask?
- What could we assume they already knew about special education?
- What can we infer about their attitudes toward higher education?
- What specific abilities will they recognize/not recognize as important in a special educator?
- What tone should we take in talking to them about special education?

Postscript

I asked that the students bring their name tags with them to class the following morning, explaining that I needed them to help me keep all their faces and names properly linked. Interestingly, the name tags reappeared at each of the remaining five sessions and were continually referred to as we discussed, worked on, and assessed the course's assignments. At the end of the course, when I asked for volunteers to donate their name tag for my files and research, no one offered. Instead, several cited their need to hang on to their tag so that they would have an example to use in adapting the activity to the special education classroom.

chapter

8

Drawing Students into Writing
A Faculty-Development Workshop

ERIC H. HOBSON

For highly visual learners like myself, sketching and doodling are often more productive prewriting, problem-solving activities than many of the invention heuristics presented in composition textbooks. The rather nondescript page from one of my notebooks (see Figure 8–1) is richer than it may appear at first glance. Doodled during a planning meeting for a series of two writing-across-the-curriculum workshops, a meeting that had lasted two hours without anyone feeling that, although we had accomplished much, it was a complete success. The first workshop would include a series of mini-lectures punctuated by active learning activities, beginning with a "fishbowl" task and ending with a "question box" writing activity that would serve as an opportunity to debrief participants. By considering this drawing, my collaborating colleague and I were able to recognize that something was missing from the record of the meeting in his notes: workshop 1 was coherent and fairly well developed; workshop 2 was still amorphous and ill-defined. Seeing this imbalance, we shifted our attention to finding a focus around which to construct the second workshop.

Drawing, not writing, had led us to a crucial insight about the structural shortcomings of the text we were developing; the drawing illustrated the incomplete relationship, in the second workshop, between ideas that seemed adequately linked when recorded in words. Nonverbal forms of communication and representation like drawing offer writers tools for discovery, planning, revision, and

138   Eric H. Hobson

Figure 8–1
WAC workshop meeting notes

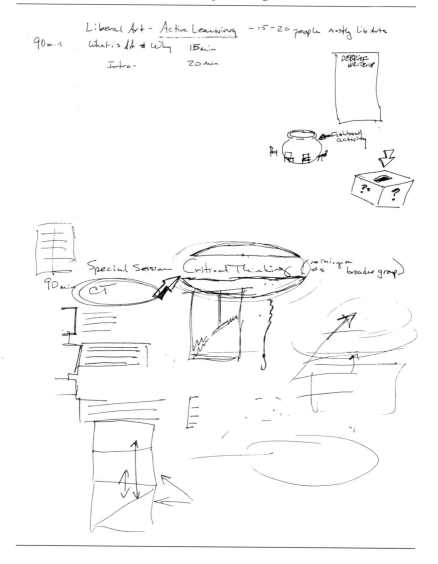

problem-solving. This is a power worth exploring at length to help
developing writers increase their communicative flexibility and effectiveness, and to explore and integrate visual activities in verbal educational settings. If teachers can recognize that they too draw and
doodle in an attempt to express meaning, even if they are not always

consciously aware of this activity or its usefulness, they have found a starting point for building visual-verbal bridges.

The previous chapters have presented many practical applications for teaching writing in a visual culture. These applications demonstrate that a visually informed approach to writing instruction has much to offer teachers in disciplines other than English. Implicit in these presentations, however, is the assumption of some level of consistent community support for such departures from the traditional, exclusively verbal language and writing class. And, make no mistake about it, community support is a decidedly important element in creating an environment that works to augment, not undermine, the visual-verbal integrations modeled in the preceding pages. Gaining the support of colleagues takes work. To help in this effort, this chapter presents an outline for a faculty development workshop designed to help teachers (principally, English and language arts teachers) see the possibilities that exist for writing instruction in using visual and visual-verbal activities.

Visual-Verbal Integration in the Writing Class

As I mentioned in Chapter 1, when I lead faculty development workshops that explore the relationship and transferability of writing and the visual arts, I usually ask participants to begin the session by taking five minutes to complete Activity 1, the "draw student X" task. And, as I noted in some detail, writing teachers at first find this task difficult, particularly for reasons linked to their own comfort and confidence in their ability to express themselves through writing and to their lack of confidence about using other forms of communication (musical or mathematical notation, for example) as effectively. The time allowed is limited, and as a result, the drawings tend to be less-than-perfect—rushed, simple, and highly idiosyncratic. These characteristics are not liabilities or limitations, however. Instead, they are exactly the responses I look for because they help me to establish several points I hope the workshop supports in theory and illustrates in practice:

- Drawing and writing involve similar processes.
- This similarity can be used to help teach many students to write more effectively.
- This strategy is particularly applicable to students whose personalities and learning styles do not mesh well with dominant methods of teaching writing.

Drawing as Process

By looking at drawing as both a tool and a process for exploring and articulating ideas, not just as a means for creating "Art," it is easier to convince writing teachers that the composing processes that drive the creation of the plastic and two-dimensional arts have much to offer students cut from various cloths. A useful observation at this point is Golden's comment that "the way in which a painter moves from sketch to completed painting could serve as an analogue for a way of progressing from draft to final paper" (1986, 59). The understanding that the composing processes across different media are similar; the basic algorithms are not as disconnected as we in the verbal fields believe. Golden's statement also supports our conviction that we need to provide a means for students to tap into their own ways of conceiving the world and translate those visions into various communicative forms, including writing.

Although we have tended to isolate drawing and writing in separate corners of the curriculum and separate corners of our lives, they are not alien, antithetical activities. Visual artists write; verbal artists draw. There has been a long history of this crossing over and cross-pollination, even if it has not always been highlighted or used as an argument for incorporating elements of both in the teaching of each. Pointing out the visual creations of artists remembered entirely for their literary efforts—such as Emily Bronte, e.e. cummings, Edgar Allan Poe, or William Faulkner—opens the minds of workshop participants to the possibility that the traditional gulf between the verbal and the visual arts is not necessarily natural. It is understandable that teachers often cling to the belief they do not have the ability to use drawing in their writing.

Worth stressing at this point in the workshop is that writers who draw and visual artists who write are using these media as tools for exploring their thinking. Our students, too, can use these alternatives to their advantage, making writing a more productive activity.

Drawing Is Invention

For the artist and the writer, invention is an essential activity. Verbal texts, like pictures and other types of visual texts, do not spring fully formed into the world. Rather, a time and a place for exploration, play, and invention help verbal and visual artists alike discover what they are trying to say and explore their options for saying it. Sketching, the visual artist's primary medium for participating in a wide variety of invention heuristics, is necessary for

- playing with initial ideas
- discovering what one already knows
- identifying gaps in one's knowledge
- developing solutions to problems
- retaining and retrieving images

By this point in the workshop we have used drawing as a form of discovery, invention, and early problem-solving, albeit within a very limited, low-risk context. I then ask workshop participants to complete Activity 2, a more stereotypical "English teacher" task. This task is alien in only one respect: participants aren't allowed to use writing while they are engaged in it. Otherwise, because they are dealing with words and the familiar task of explaining grammar and mechanics, it is perceived as fairly accessible and only moderately risky.

The drawings that result from Activity 2 are often cursory, basic, rough, and highly idiosyncratic. Most responses resemble the example in Figure 8–2 which represents the concept "parallelism."

As rudimentary as these drawings are, however, they have much to offer on a number of levels:

1. **Workshop:** By sharing these drawings, participants experience success in explaining highly abstract, even arbitrary, features of language without using a single word. For many of us, this is quite a revelation.

2. **Individual/Personal:** Teachers need to experience visual activities of this sort in order to gain confidence that they can use visuals. They also need to feel the different levels of comfort/

Activity 2

TASK: Doodle a picture or a description of one of the following grammatical errors or problems:

comma splice	split infinitive	subject/verb disagreement
fused sentence	misplaced modifiers	mixed metaphors
possessives	parallelism	double negative
tense shifts	person shifts	repetition

TIME: 10 minutes
TIPS: Sketch quickly
        Trust your instincts
        Make changes: perfectionist impulses are limiting
GOAL: Regardless of how primitive the drawing, try to be able to explain the resulting visual text to another person.

Figure 8–2
"Parallelism"

discomfort students experience when they are asked to use media for which they have little skill or history of success.

3. **Teachers:** Activities like this offer teachers alternative and specific ways to help visual learners and concrete thinkers understand the abstract rules of grammar and usage they encounter in class and in their textbooks. Building from this base, they can create visual-verbal bridges for these learners.

Drawing Aids Revision

Revision is the most difficult aspect of the composing process to teach. I preach the virtue and value of revision as *the* essential tool in the writer's toolbox, but, I am never quite convinced that my students value revision much beyond my course. I find Golden's (1986) words somewhat comforting: "Often when college students are asked to revise their drafts, they insert, delete, or change material without considering the effect on the entire composition. Current approaches to revision, although beneficial, frequently remain too abstract for Introductory Composition students who cannot recognize the absence of harmonious connections between paragraphs or identify expressions that might convey a vague meaning to a reader" (59).

Perhaps the abstract nature of my discussion of revision—the how and the why—fails to achieve the desired effect with my students. A much more tangible approach is to engage students in the revision process through drawing, a medium that they can see and physically manipulate. Using that awareness as a starting point, there are a number of ways to apply strategies and algorithms developed by visual artists to help student writers learn to control the process more productively.

Activity 3 (and, in conjunction, Activity 4 and Activity 5) provides one strategy for introducing revision in a systematic, tangible way, one that leaves a record of the steps taken and the decisions that prompted them.

Many writers—especially those who function in a concrete operational way—have difficulty dealing with the abstract nature of the activities we ask them to undertake in a writing course, even tasks as easy as "tell me how you got here." Sketching events allows struggling writers to

- deal more effectively with chronological time
- make the abstract concrete
- pin down fleeting images and memories for further reflection and development

In addition, sketching provides composition teachers a convenient and inclusive forum for discussing and modeling abstract revision strategies. Reporting on one teacher's use of drawing in an elementary language arts classroom to encourage better writing, Ernst (1996) notes that "Darcy concentrated on helping her third graders understand the connection between picture making and revision. She discovered that once a picture was revised, her students naturally revised their writing about the picture as well. Revision is literally re-seeing; a picture makes this difficult skill concrete" (147).

Activity 4 demonstrates the validity of this observation and its applicability.

Activity 3

TASK: Draw a storyboard of at least six one-frame cartoons that
        recounts "My Trip to This Workshop Site."
TIME: 15 minutes
TIPS: Sketch quickly
        Trust your lines—the sketches are "writer-based" and must
           make sense only to you
        Go for a broad overview rather than minute detail
        Emphasize the sequence of events
GOAL: Be able to describe the event to someone else using *only* your
        sketches.

Reluctant writers of all ages often face potential writer's blocks
that reinforce their apprehension about their writing abilities and
reenergize their resistance to taking any risks, especially the type of
risk from which learning moments arise. As it is, many are pleased to
survive the first draft and do not intend to go through the process
again. When it comes to revising their initial drafts, they have trouble
seeing their texts from the perspective of a potential reader who
needs details that support the author's claims in order to come to
agreement with the author's thesis. These writers need help in learning to recognize the types of details that readers appreciate having
available as they read. Sketching provides an alternative to yet another lecture about the need for details and illustrative examples in
successful texts.

One of the most useful aspects of Activity 4 is that, in completing
the directions as given, students must consciously consider their ini-

Activity 4

TASK: Use the storyboard to plan a narrative rendition of your journey to today's workshop.

STEPS IN THE PROCESS:

  1. Separate frames/sections and, for effect, rearrange in something
      other than strict chronological time.
  2. Delete any frames that are not absolutely necessary to the narra-
      tive.
  3. Add any details or resketch any frames where more information is
      available/needed/relevant.
  4. Insert any needed words to act as memory prompts.

TIME: 10 minutes
TIPS: Storyboards (grids) with at least six (6) distinct drawing spaces
         work best
         Sketch quickly and confidently
         The images need only make sense to you

---

tial sketches in terms of missing information. For many visual learners, looking at their emerging "text" while it remains in visual form
allows them to recognize important details they have overlooked, assumed were obvious, or only just remembered. Once they recognize
the problem, most writers—and all workshop participants—go back to
their sketches to add needed information. Workshop discussion can
focus on the ease with which one can segue from this revision task to
written texts.

Olson (1992) suggests a further step to help students identify and
provide the types of additional information readers need. She asks
students to engage in any of the following "special effects" tasks:
drawing from a strange point of view, drawing gradual transforma-
tions or metamorphoses, or "zoom" drawings (36). I find the "zoom,"
close-up task particularly apt as a tool to develop awareness of how
to create that level of detail. I have used this type of drawing repeat-
edly with students in writing classes and with clients in the writing
center. Within the workshop setting, however, I require participants
to take part of one of their drawings in Activity 4 and do a close-up.
(see Activity 5).

The previous activities take workshop participants through most
of the writing process, but in a less familiar medium. Only when they
have completed Activity 3 and 4 (Activity 5, too, when I decide there

Activity 5

TASK: 1. Choose one panel from your narrative about getting to this workshop and, in the space provided below, zoom in on the most important or most interesting part of the scene. Draw this part of the panel in as much detail as you can.

2. When you complete the close-up, list the specific details you included in the drawing.

TIME: 15 minutes

is time to include it), do I allow them to translate their narrative into written form. By delaying their use of verbal communicative tools, I hope that the workshop participants

- experience how it feels for their students to attempt complex communicative tasks in unfamiliar mediums

- recognize that a writing-based invention and revision activity is not the exclusive way to create a first draft

- consider experimenting with visual composing activities alongside standard activities in language arts and writing-across-the-curriculum classes

Conclusion

What is it about a drawing that can unlock a storehouse of past experience? By returning to images I have drawn, I am more likely to remember snippets of conversation, the movements and reactions of people, and the mood of the surrounding environment. Images offer learners like me a "thicker" record of past events.

Although a predilection for images fits the learning styles profile of visually dependent people, mounting evidence from cognitive research bolsters my belief that visually based activity offers all students a way to make their writing processes more flexible and efficient. Much of human cognition is imagistic and impressionistic, more linked to general gestalts than to specific words. Visual images lie at the root of human thought and subsequent communication. This model intuitively makes sense because images would seem to be more compact and efficient storage units than words. Supporting this intuitive leap, Sereno's research into the origins of human language use suggests that visual images serve as the base for a logical reason: the *wiring* in the brain that produces language is built on long-standing visual processing systems put to new use (for more on Sereno's research, see Chapter 6).

As the discussions in the preceding chapters have demonstrated, integrating visual elements into instruction across the curriculum affords benefits to all involved. We are convinced that carefully articulated and constructed uses of visually enhanced pedagogy are extremely powerful teaching and learning tools. As Shuman and Wolfe remind us, "It is the galvanizing of thought through the use of any form of creative endeavor that contributes to learning; ideally, then, students should be permitted access to all of these composing, meaning-making processes. In a classroom where students are encouraged and permitted to use many different forms of composing and creating, the potential for learning seems greater than in classrooms where only limited forms are employed or allowed" (4–5).

Response

JOAN A. MULLIN

The Workshop as Classroom
and Classroom as Workshop

In reading Eric's chapter, I kept thinking about applying his drawing activities in my own and in colleagues' classes across the disciplines. Likewise, I thought of using the same drawing techniques to involve teachers and faculty in my writing and WAC workshops. So what I responded to most in this chapter (besides the fact that it's fun) is the following:

- *The activities are hands-on.* Whether running a workshop or a classroom, for faculty or for students, I find experiential learning the most powerful means for introducing new ideas or skills. Eric's activities can work spontaneously with a minimum of resources or with elaborate preparation; the methods can be part of a syllabus, but anyone could also take advantage of the "teachable moment," asking students/faculty to take out a sheet of paper and start drawing—now!

- *The activities are transferable.* I can think of many ways to use the exercises to "draw" out and draw in students at all levels. After working with colleagues who teach elementary school, high school, or college, I have begun to see how drawing, like writing strategies, can work across levels to motivate and teach abstract or concrete concepts. When Eric's "draw the grammatical/mechanical rule" is used in a multidisciplinary setting, teachers discover that we all forget the "rules," that the reasons are sometimes easier to draw than to articulate, and that once drawn, they are easier to articulate. Likewise, students (as well as teachers) learn that drawing helps them think through a concept, or it shows them—vividly—that they really don't know what they thought they did. From there, learning can take place.

- *Some of the exercises help teach revision,* one of the most challenging aspects of textual production in any discipline. I intensely dislike many aspects of revision, and that's probably one reason I insist on it with my students, and (like Eric) it's also probably why I have sometimes taught it unsuccessfully: It is difficult to teach well what you yourself don't like to do. The drawing activities open up another way of visualizing my work, and another way for me to visualize and talk to students about their work. As Eric points out, working in a writing center has taught us the value of mapping, grouping, drawing, and other visualization strategies.

Thematic Variations

Planned or Flexible

These writing activities can be spontaneously adapted by a teacher during class or carefully planned and integrated into existing syllabi. I recently planned to incorporate the storyboard into a course on teaching writing across disciplines and levels but (unexpectedly) used the grammar sketch one day when we were discussing the use of writing conventions in light of dialect, language learning, and definitions of literacy. The planned storyboard likewise produced some surprising results during a faculty workshop on visuals and classroom practice, though I used the idea to produce different ends (see below). Like many of the practices in this book, these activities are flexible enough to complement disciplinary objectives, motivational enough to enliven a dull classroom and reach the day's learning objective, and adaptable to long-range curricular goals: the storyboard can work as an organizing tactic for students developing and researching projects over the course of a semester.

Across Levels

Eric has focused on the importance of creating a collegial group that encourages new pedagogy. After doing a workshop with Eric in which he went through these exercises with faculty, I began to look for ways in which I could create such a community and draw a group of faculty to using visuals in their classrooms. Excited by the thought, I volunteered for a Friday morning presentation on the use of visuals in the classroom before I had really thought the project through. Stumped, I asked myself how visuals work across the curriculum. Would the astronomy faculty member care about punctuation, or the biologist care about revision? (I knew the humanists and social scientists would!)

The one common visual denominator we all rely on is the drawing given us in textbooks. The writing center collects assignments and textbooks from classes in order to work with the students, and I paged through them, copying a few visuals from each text.

The day of the presentation, using an overhead projector, I displayed the visuals, which I had arranged in order of least to most confusing (to me) one by one. As we examined the visual and the accompanying text, small gasps were audible in the audience as faculty discovered in one case that a common trajectory drawn in a physics textbook was incorrect, and in another case, that the table in a political science text was missing a column of information. Sometimes fortune smiles on the ignorant presenter; what I as an outsider had gathered as examples of visuals I found confusing turned out to be confusing for more reasons than I could have foreseen. As faculty began their discussion of what we had discovered, we began to talk about our blind reliance on visual information: on how we don't question what may (or may not) be before our eyes. It was easy to move from a discussion of how visuals could deceive—though they should be helpful—to how we could use visuals in our teaching.

Near the end of my presentation, I introduced Eric's third exercise, by asking faculty to draw six panels explaining how they got to the workshop. Through much comfortable kidding about our lack of colored pencils and some attention devoted to faculty who worked with their tongues sticking out, participants began in midsketch to see how drawing processes could be useful in their classrooms. A sociologist commented that students had a difficult time understanding the varied steps by which grassroots organizations come to power: drawing these steps in a flow chart would show options and alternative routes. A political scientist also used the flow chart idea for students designing a database, not really an original thought, but one he hadn't used because he hadn't seen its value. A physicist decided that before referring students to textbook pictures, he would have them draw their own trajectories, and perhaps even create their own "word pictures" as problems for other students to solve. In each case, the idea was local, contextual, related to one particular classroom—but it opened up other possibilities for colleagues. Eric's workshop had given me the idea for the presentation to begin with and his storyboard produced a broad range of ideas for professors in their classrooms.

In a similar situation, teachers taking a writing-across-levels-and-disciplines class (teachers of children in grades two through twelve) were asked to do Eric's grammar rule exercise. As they struggled with both the drawing and the interpretation, we began to talk about Mina Shaughnessy's work with basic writers. Teachers wondered if their students (especially younger students) would be able to use drawing to express rules they had constructed prior to entering school, rules based on oral speech, which didn't translate to written communication, or rules that governed dialects rather than academic English. One of the second grade teachers suggested that her students might draw the grammar rules and compile them into a book for next year's students; another teacher thought that her fourth-grade students might be able to compile a similar book for second graders as part of their "community service" project.

Meanwhile, curious to see what would happen in my composition class if students were asked to draw their most common grammar or sentence "problem," I asked my students to humor me by doing so. Of course what resulted was a half-finished series of drawings as many of the students asked in frustration, "How can I draw it if I don't know how to do it?" That in turn led to a discussion not only of rules but of ways students remember or proofread for certain writing conventions.

Besides working as a method for creating a narrative, Eric's storyboard idea is another way to analyze a picture or a graphic or media presentation. Students often deny that they are manipulated by commercials, news programs, or even MTV. They claim that they already know the media controls, tricks, and draws reviewers into a trap. Yet, when asked to reproduce their "favorite" commercials in storyboard panels, from memory, students were surprised at what they couldn't remember: the setting, the colors, the name of the product. One of two things tends to happen: they remember peripheral pieces of an ad or a commercial, or they remember little except the large main parts of the ad or commercial. I then asked them to draw a storyboard while watching the commercial or the ad. Invariably, students watch again and again, and begin to discover subtle cues they had not "seen" before but to which they have obviously been exposed and have registered unconsciously. Such a task leads students to cultural analysis, textual analysis, or creating effective visuals for communication.

Revision, "Re-vision"

We tell students to look again, reread, proof, revise, but many of them, pressed for time, do "just enough" and miss the point of lifelong learning. To "re-vision," means to look again, to think about what is missing and what is there, to anticipate how another might see and interpret so you, in turn, can again "re-vision" its presentation. Getting outside one's own personal knowledge of a paper is very difficult during the best of times, but it is especially so when there is little time to put a text down, let it sit, and then pick it up again. The storyboard, narrative, and zoom, the last in particular, give students the distance they need during this all-important stage of production. I'm trying to avoid the word "writing" here, because I have seen the storyboard work when students need to create a visual product: when they create a plan, write about it, zoom in on its parts, and then restructure their original idea. This works in art history design classes, but it is also what the political science professor saw as a potential resource for students working with data bases, or the biology professor for students designing hypotheses and experiments to test them, or the history professor for students tracing and charting their family tree.

Picturing a structure, seeing ideas in a spatial arrangement, and then focusing on one part at a time, creates a less painful medium for many students. Drawing proves especially valuable in student conferences or writing center tutorials. In trying to understand a paper's organization, you can have them draw the paper in sections, or if you choose, you can draw your version of what you have read. This often leads to a clearer view of the glitches, bare spaces, lack of evidence, needless repetition, places in which the writer/designer is speaking only to him or herself. Since the difficulty of revision is to get out of our own heads, drawing the structure of our papers or zooming up close on our details can put the words or design that exists in "perfect" order in our heads in true perspective. It can help us "re-vision."

Postscript

Our responses to these chapters revealed to us, even as we composed them, how much using visuals has already permeated our own classrooms. Much to our delight, we also encountered colleagues (besides those presented here) who have discovered the effectiveness of visuals in teaching. Just as writing across the curriculum stresses that writing should be folded into the curriculum, we have found ways in which visuals can be part of our teaching methodology. We also found ourselves focusing more and more on how to "read," analyze, and create effective visuals. We believe, like Gunter Kress and others who write on the subject, that all the evidence around us shows that visuals no longer just augment text; now, the text augments the visuals. To ignore the visual evidence, or worse, to ignore our students' needs—to respond intelligently to and produce visuals—is to antiquate this thing we value most: reading, interpreting and communicating in all their forms, the forms we have now, and the ones yet to come.

Bibliography

Adams, R. L. 1985. "Aesthetic Dialogue for Children: Paradigm and Program." *Art Education* 38 (5): 12–15.

Berger, J. 1972. *Ways of Seeing.* London: Penguin.

Cleaver, B. P., P. Scheurer, and M. E. Shorey. 1993. "Architectural Images Through the Dual Lens of Picture Books and Creative Dramatics." *International Visual Literacy Association Proceedings.* IVLA.

Coulmas, F. 1988. *The Writing Systems of the World.* Cambridge, MA: Basil Blackwell.

Dunn, R., and K. Dunn. 1978. *Teaching Students Through Their Individual Learning Styles: A Practical Approach.* Reston, VA: Reston Publishing.

Eisner, E. W. 1997. "Cognition and Representation: A Way to Pursue the American Dream." *Phi Delta Kappan* 78 (5): 349–53.

Ernst, K. 1994. *Picturing Learning: Artists and Writers in the Classroom.* Portsmouth, NH: Heinemann.

Farrell-Childers, P., A. R. Gere, and A. Young, eds. 1994. *Programs and Practices: Writing Across the Secondary School Curriculum.* Portsmouth, NH: Boynton/Cook.

Fleming, N. D., and C. Mills. 1992. "Not Another Inventory, Rather a Catalyst for Reflection." *To Improve the Academy* 11: 137–55.

Foote, S. 1974. "Stars in Their Courses." In *The Civil War: A Narrative.* Vol. 2. New York: Random House.

Gardner, H. 1983. *Frames of Mind: The Theory of Multiple Intelligences.* New York: Basic Books.

Golden, C. 1986. "Composition: Writing and the Visual Arts." *Journal of Aesthetic Education* 20 (3): 59–68.

Gordon, T. 1996. "Drawing My Selves Together: An Editor's Notebook." In *New Entries: Learning by Writing and Drawing,* edited by R. S. Hubbard and K. Ernst, 150–57. Portsmouth, NH: Heinemann.

Graves, M. 1977. "The Necessity for Drawing: Tangible Speculation." *Architectural Design* 6: 384–94.

Gutin, J. A. 1996. "A Brain That Talks." *Discover* 17 (6): 83–90.

Harris, R. 1986. *The Origin of Writing.* Peru, IL: Open Court.

Harste, J. C., V. A. Woodward, and C. L. Burke. 1986. *Language Stories and Literacy Lessons.* Portsmouth, NH: Heinemann.

Hjerter, K. G. 1986. *Doubly Gifted: The Author as Visual Artist.* New York: Harry N. Abrams.

Hobson, E. H. 1990. "The Writer's Journal and the Artist's Sketchpad." *Writing Lab Newsletter* 14 (1): 1–3, 14.

Hubbard, R. S., and K. Ernst, eds. 1996. *New Entries: Learning by Writing and Drawing.* Portsmouth, NH: Heinemann.

Jean, G. 1992. *Writing: The Story of Alphabets and Scripts.* New York: Harry N. Abrams.

Jensen, G., and J. DiTiberio. 1989. *Personality and the Teaching of Composition.* Norwood, NJ: Ablex.

Keefe, J. W., and J. S. Monk. 1986. *Learning Style Profile.* Reston, VA: The National Association of Secondary School Principals.

Klee, P. 1962. *On Modern Art.* Translated by P. Findlay. London: Faber and Faber.

Kress, G., and T. VanLeeuwen. 1996. *Reading Images: The Grammar of Visual Design.* London: Routledge.

Lawrence, G. D. 1993. *People Types and Tiger Stripes.* Gainesville: Center for Application of Psychological Types, Inc.

Lowry, M. 1996. *CPS Portfolio Project.* Classroom Assignment. Chattanooga, TN: The McCallie School.

Lowry, M., and P. Childers. 1997. "Empowering Students to Design Assessments in Science." *The Clearing House.* Special Edition: 97–102.

Matthews, D. B. 1996. "An Investigation of Learning Styles and Perceived Academic Achievement for High School Students." *The Clearing House* 69 (4): 249–54.

Mullin, J. A. 1994. "Feminist Theory, Feminist Pedagogy: The Gap Between What We Say and What We Do." *Composition Studies* 24 (2): 13–23.

Myers, I. B. 1990. *Gifts Differing.* 2d ed. Palo Alto: Consulting Psychologist Press.

NCTE. "NCTE to You." 1997. *College English* 59 (1): 97–104.

Neuhardt-Minor, C. 1994. "Words and Images." In *Programs and Practices: Writing Across the Secondary School Curriculum,* edited by P. Farrell-Childers, A. R. Gere, and A. Young, 211–13. Portsmouth, NH: Boynton/Cook.

Nickel, L. 1994. "Writing and Pre-Calculus." In *Programs and Practices: Writing Across the Secondary School Curriculum,* edited by P. Farrell-Childers, A. R. Gere, and A. Young, 200–204. Portsmouth, NH: Boynton/Cook.

Olson, J. L. 1992. *Envisioning Writing: Toward an Integration of Drawing and Writing.* Portsmouth, NH: Heinemann.

Perkinson, D. B. *Seeing the Difference in the Math Classroom.* Unpublished paper.

Scholes, R. 1989. *Protocols of Reading.* New Haven: Yale University Press.

Shaughnessy, M. 1977. *Errors and Expectations.* New York: Oxford University Press.

Shuman, R. B., and D. Wolfe. 1990. *Teaching English Through the Visual Arts: Theory and Research into Practice (TRIP) Series.* Urbana, IL: NCTE.

Wilmerding, J. 1987. *Andrew Wyeth: The Helga Pictures.* New York: Harry N. Abrams.

Left to right: Joan Mullin, Eric Hobson, Pam Childers

Pamela B. Childers: I remember when my grandfather and I searched for broken robins' eggs and blue jay feathers in the grass of my childhood yard. Colors, shapes, landscapes, and two Renoir prints on my bedroom walls were my world of reading, writing, and imagining. That visual environment led to years of stories, poems, and degrees in biology, English, writing, secondary education, writing across the disciplines, and adult education. My husband Malcolm's lessons on how to see as an artist have given me new ways of seeing my writing in a different format (photography). I still immerse myself in my visual surroundings—living walls of Malcolm's art, a real view from our mountain home, a writing center filled with art posters, landscape photographs, and a wall of windows overlooking Chattanooga and the mountains beyond. Whether I live within the historically steeped structural designs and greyed colors of London or New York, the pastoral lush greens of New Zealand and Ireland, the soothing ocean blues of Martha's Vineyard and Maui, or the desert sage, orange, and brown of the Four Corners, the visual culture continues to stimulate my reading, conjuring new learning activities, and writing. Each day brings ideas for new and different writing workshops with the visual arts.

Eric H. Hobson: The grandfather I never met was an artist, and I think that may be one reason for my parents signing me up to take art lessons one summer. Although those lessons were short-lived, I think that in combination with genetic agents, they played a role in who I am. I came to my current teaching position as assistant professor of English in a circuitous manner. Stumbling into an undergraduate English program because it offered a one-quarter earlier graduation date than did majors in art history or studio art, I doodled and sketched my way through the Ph.D. specializing in composition. Since then I have put my visual talents to work teaching writing and in developing and administering writing centers and writing-across-the-curriculum programs. Although reconciled to the fact that a career as a professional artist is not in the offing, I continue to draw (especially during committee meetings) and paint whenever I can make free time in my schedule as a teacher, father, and faculty developer.

Joan A. Mullin: Our household was the proud purchaser of a *New World Book Encyclopedia* in the 1950s, and I was fascinated by the visuality of the alphabetical writing in the beginning of each volume: Sumarian, Phoenician, Greek, Roman. So even before I could really read, I spent hours copying down the forms in columns, figuring that when I had finished, I would be able to write (speak) in all those languages—even prior to being able to write in my own. From there I took to sketching pictures from the *World Book,* sketching objects in my room or outside, but it was all very covert because such things were not known in my culture or class—nor were they encouraged. Reading was—which is why I took to creating metaphoric and colorful pictures in my head. This proved an acceptable substitute to all concerned, especially since school schedules left no time for anything other than Latin, world history, economics, and literature. Nonetheless, I would pick up sketching pads now and then, draw for my children, and, finally, had the opportunity to work in a writing-intensive art history design class—a venture so successful that the faculty member and I have continued to do so for five years. This, and my reading on the intersections of art and language take me right back to my beginnings.